WINGS THAT SPREAD

WINGS THAT SPREAD

RAMESH SANGLE

PARTRIDGE

A Penguin Random House Company

To order additional copies of this book, contact
Partridge India
000 800 10062 62
orders.india@partridgepublishing.com

www.partridgepublishing.com/india

I am humble as individual self in presence of the divine in any form including outward expression.

PREFACE

All Characters' names, situations are imaginary.

There is no intention to hurt anybody for their profession, business or people in common.

This is a simple imaginary novel (a work of fiction), involves human nature and their relations and affections despite religion.

No country, place or event in this story is intended as a reference to any person, place or country.

Democracy or socialism is the way of life like an individual religion all over. If any of such above may find any similarity then that is just a coincidence and needs to be ignored. Some highest expressions are years old published in news paper column. I also offer my profound gratitude to my friends and others for their generous assistance for this book.

Author: Ramesh N. Sangle,
Mumbai.

Its' early dawn when brighter stars getting silently deemed but on the Western horizon Venus is still cool but bright, like newly wedded Queen.

Jessica Macmillan in her 40's, is on the terrace of the 14th storied tower built by herself, from where one can have a complete view around. She is called as "J.M." by most of the town people. She is a loveable and popular personality. Basically not much social but her profession and nature made her so. With deep brown eyes, light brown hair around her shoulder, of medium height, she is looking graceful in a pink rich gown. She keeps looking at those beautiful colorful leaves and flowers around. Those saplings which she brought from various nurseries from distant villages, in her busy schedule. Among those entire she like the heart shape dark green leaves with pink star at its center, spreading veins around the most. She takes care of every plant like a tiny child, for which she has all accessories, tools like scissor, trowel, chisel and cutter, small hammer to make different boxes and shelter to protect small creepers from hot sun rays and icy winter.

Sun is yet to arise from the east-side, from beyond the sloppy mountains. It is cool early morning at about

6 O'clock. Greenery on and around mountain getting brighter and golden as east end horizon is getting alive. Jessica has brought coffee trolley with coffee tray from kitchen. She always uses white coffee pot with Golden mug to match her coffee and bring to usual table surrounded by three chairs.

It is April end, ice on the verge of molten, and indicating spring time, where small green shoots are protruding out all over.

She seats down with hot coffee, quiet as if meditating with nature and suddenly observed light orange sunrise. "Amazing!" she exclaims with sudden surge of freshness felt deep inside. "Am I myself with nature or a part of nature?". She puts down her coffee pot and stands up. She then looks at West which is still dark, but can spot high rise of 40 floors; four towers at very center of the market, designed and built up by her own associate company under her leadership.

Town people always look upon her as a great architect and a highly ambitious woman who looks as young as in her 30's.

Her broad and kind hearted nature keeps her young though she is much older. This 14 floor tower is at extreme East end, at periphery of the township. She is today proudly standing in her terrace-balcony. This is the time she remembers her past 30 years, her life till now and her beautiful childhood.

She was born in a village of about a thousand people population, mainly farmers and craftsmen leading a happy life. Her father Samuel was a small farmer who visited the bigger town by his small horse drawn cart to sell milk and vegetables. Before returning home he used to purchase his daily requirements from the main market.

He had a small one storey wooden house, with small garden around. Though he was staying alone, he maintained everything as it was when his parents were alive. He had constructed small out—house for his farm tools and had developed interest in construction work also. Whenever he was visiting various towns, he could notice day to day development and was curious about plenty of building material spread around.

Every season his 20 Acre farm was giving him a good yield of barley, maize and seasonal vegetable. Patrick's farm was adjacent to Samuel's farm. Patrick had seen many ups and downs of Samuel's family. His father was an ex-warrior, who had fought in second war and died on the battle field. Samuel's mother could not sustain that shock and died. Thus Samuel had become an orphan when he was eighteen. He was suddenly burdened with the responsibility of his family farm, and so had to abandon his studies.

Then Patrick started helping him. Whenever he was in need, right from getting equipment required for farming,. giving his tractor to plough the field, paying for oil required to run engine, lending him water pump set whenever Samuel's pump needed to be repaired and so on.

It was a rainy day. Patrick's house stood on the border of his paddy crop field. On the other side was Samuel's farm. Patrick came to Samuel's farm house with his sick horse. "What's wrong sir" Samuel asked.

"My horse is sick, unable to walk; he has not eaten for many days. But I want to save him. Can you take care of him? All my workers have fled away and only two are left with me who know nothing about the stud. The servants, who ran away, have also stolen some costly equipment from store room."

"Oh, that's very bad. However, I will treat this pony. He looks quite a steed! Do not worry, within a few days I will make him healthy and strong by feeding maize with honey and mixed with orange juice." Samuel was speaking confidently but Patrick was apprehensive. However, the horse really recovered within a week. Patrick was amazed and grateful to Samuel. Then another incident was took place before setting of winter. About 200 horses of Patrick were grazing on the out skirt of the village at the slope of the mountain leading to the valley. It so happened that Samuel was driving his horse cart full of Jungle wood and was going to a saw—mill nearby, to get it cut in plain planks, to cover his house roof and sides before winter. While driving he noticed this big herd of horses belonging to Patrick. Some of the horses had metallic brass neck chains and most of them were dark brown. Some unknown 4to5 persons were leading away this herd in suspicious manner to the valley from where he was coming. Immediately he halted, untied his horse from cart. Removed long sturdy rope from plank and long spear headed iron rod. Then he mounted the horse and rode near to the thieves who without much resistance ran away, which surprised him. He thought probably they may not be professionals and had taken the advantage of the horse keeper's absence. He galloped towards the valley to chase the thieves but in vein. On returning he took all of the horses back to Patrick, who was sick and laying on his bed since morning. His two workers were away in town to purchase needful.

Samuel did not tell him all that happened but asked his servant to get a doctor from town. As soon as Patrick recovered Samuel narrated the entire episode and asked him to employ more care-takers. All this brought Samuel more and more closer to Patrick. Patrick developed confidence in Samuel and soon proposed for his daughter Jennifer to Samuel, who accepted without any hesitation, and then Samuel and Jennifer got married. Though Jennifer and Samuel were staying neighbors since childhood, they spoke occasionally, and never had any attraction toward each other. In spite of this, after accepting each other they enjoyed their married life thoroughly, and never had anything to keep them apart. Jennifer was from a very rich back—ground. Once married, they were as if made for each other. Jennifer worked with Samuel every day. She never left him alone even in field work. Even her father appreciated her as a self-made girl, and thought that she could make Samuel's life pleasurable and also prosperous. He was proud of his daughter. Days passed on. Sam and Jenny had two kids. One son, named as Jack and the daughter named as Jessica, When Jennifer and Samuel were in the field, sawing seeds, watering, etc their kids used to be with them. They too learnt hard work. Little daughter Jessica used to bring some cheese toast and tea to their parents in field. She never lost any opportunity to help her parents.

Both the kids enjoyed perfect village life, with different paddy crops, vegetables and fruits around their farm, and also the little rivulet and various trees and birds. Jessica's brother use to catch small colorful birds, give them little fish stock which was his catch and even some berries etc. and so. They grew and entered the school. There too they made many friends and enjoyed different games. The school had more discipline and greater freedom for self activities.

Jennifer and Samuel were very particular about their development and studies.

Patrick use to love Jack as he was good sportsman. He was very fond of football. When he was eleven he got many prizes while playing with different school. Most of his free time passed on football ground, either participating or arranging games and matches. Jessica was, fair well featured, with sparkling eyes—deep brown and light brown hair. Comparatively she had less friends but she had natural talent to sketch and paint. Over the period she started loving dance. Her teacher too found her natural beauty and talent. Creative minded Jessica could easily form tiny figures of dogs out of clay—mould. When teacher noticed her art she gave her plaster of Paris powder and taught her how to make small statues, with it.

Life was going on in simple but beautiful manner. For Jessica everyday was like blooming of a new flower, and night like a warm shielding her in wooden house.

—xxxx—

A luxurious Bus swiftly entered school premises. The well dressed driver stepped down from bus and straight went to principal's office. The village schools building were moderate with sloppy roof of cement asbestos sheet. Each class room had beautiful carved doors.

This was second successful time where Jessica was selected for dance competition and was to go to the city with other members from the school to perform a ballet. Her elder brother too went along with his friends to cheer up her on stage. Last year Jessica had performed in a group. They were trained by a teacher who was once a good ballet dancer. She used to perform for hours on end, and her name was among top dancers. She could attract crowds to fill the whole auditorium. But because of some tragedy in her life she had to leave everything behind and joined the school as dance teacher. Her teaching helped to master the dance form. Her devotion and her teacher's passion to teach her had brought silver medal to the school last year. Now she was aiming for the Gold and had put in tireless efforts.

The ballet was choreographed after long deliberation. It was a classic French theme in English version. Jessica loved this and while performing the Ballet she forgot everything else. Today once again she had boarded the bus to go to the competition. To her surprise, many villagers surrounded bus to wish this 15 year young pretty and ambitious girl. All cheered her as the bus moved. After two hours the bus reached the auditorium where she was to perform. The hall was delightfully lit up in a combination of colors thrown on stage. She went to dressing room. Her brother helped her to unload her luggage and waited till she dressed up. Then he joined his friends who were sitting in the auditorium, of about 700 persons capacity. Front raw was reserved for V.I.P.s and cultural minister who the guest of honor. A special team of judges was also present. Beams of light blue and orange—colure light were thrown on the stage to achieve a special effect.

. The 1st performer of the day was from highly status school of the same town. The ballet performance was the main attraction for packed house. Expensively dressed, French-couples—slowly entered on stage to welcome applause of the audience with grace. Drum bits sounded and instruments started playing. Audience was nearly hypnotized in their seats. As the Ballet progressed the every minute was thrilled with different steps. After 40 minutes of performance, the group of status school was given standing ovation. Three more performances of Russian, Japanese, and Rumania dances were presented. Now the turn was of the village school group. They were introduced and announced as the quality performer and winner of the silver medal of last year. The audience was also told that Jessica was a wonder of a wonder girl who was to perform now. Jessica, smart and neat, nicely featured with light brown hair entered staged with high jump like an angel. Audience was stunned to see her flying like on wings in the sky and then controlling her self—she came down like a pigeon on the stage. Everyone exclaimed. Hand-Clapping continued for long time. Audience sat down with a sigh. Drums and Musicians missed the moment and could not even catch her steps but went unnoticed because of the concentration was fully on Jessica who proved to be a real wonder-girl. Beautiful long hands swinging in the air was real attraction.

The professional musicians had to co-ordinate with her steps. Other dancers too found it difficult to match her step. Sensing this she slowly managed to co-ordinate her moves with others. The Ballet continued with melodious music. Its, slow, quick, normal and again rapid steps were keeping audience glued to their chairs. They even forget to clap. They were unaware how nearly two Hours passed and woke up with a jerk when the Ballet was over. And standing ovation was given, which was approval from the judges too! Jessica's group had won the Gold-Medal. Though ballet troop went back to back-room—her teacher, trainer, brother, friends, everybody rushed to congratulate Jessica and have a close look at her. She was again called back on the stage to accept greetings from crowd.

"It's Jessica own Gold Medal".

They also given her name as

"Wonder Girl from Village town."

Audience once again clapped. Cameras flashed and Trumpets—and Drums exploded in musical applause. The second prize went to the so called high-Status school. Puncturing their false pride. The audience continued to applause and shouting "Jessica-! Jessica-!" all around the auditorium. She was hurriedly taken to their Bus along with other members. Her brother collected all her belongings and greetings, bouquets in a basket. Jessica sat near the Bus door to give glimpses to the crowd. Meanwhile a boy who had staged for the high status school came running in his school's blue uniform with a orange daffodil in his hand. She recognized him and stretched her hand towards him. Security man helped him to get near door and to present to Jessica that Daffodil with shaky hand. As bus moved forward she waved affectionately to him.

Though the success of Gold medal was not a miracle. Her surge of sudden action which was out of act on stage put her on top. Momentary her group of dancers and musicians had hard time to synchronize with her. Her teacher too appreciated her initiative who could not teach that because of her twisted ankle.

It was almost midnight when the bus approached the village border; everyone was taken by surprise to see a big Arch erected with heavy lighting. Colorful lamps were lit near the entrance of the arch and music played on speaker created as if fair or Xmas celebration. All villagers of the township had lined up at both end of road. As Jessica alighted from bus along with other members bugle sounded. The Band master given signal to other drummers. Jessica and her troupe were led to the school premises followed by all villagers. Everybody lined up on school ground. Villagers took their seats around to witness the occasion. School's anthem was sung proudly. The principal, and all other teachers gave three cheers to Jessica, saying—"Jessica", our—"Wonder-Girl we are proud of you !"—. The principal said "Now Jessica's name will be written in golden letter. "Some one in crowd had already envisaged this and had brought one banner written in gold "JESSICA, A WONDER-GIRL!" Jessica's parent were asked to hold this banner aloft and people gathered around burst in joy and there was clap of thunder. Her father Samuel, mother Jennifer and grandfather Patrick embraced her affectionately after giving her a bunch of flowers.

—xxx—

Jessica was disturbed as her peon rang the terrace bell to bring a tray of toasts and coffee. She allowed him to arrange it on the table. He had also came with message that some office attendant wants her to have appointment with some civil contractors, who was in charge of sculpture design to finalize the construction of a prestigious monument.

This project was very important to her which will be erected in the main the city.

"Oh! but she was not in a mood to finalize the appointment and asked her servant to hold it till she say's yes!"

It was 9 o'clock. Sun was up and the mist was disappearing. She sat down to have a break fast. She made strong coffee and sipped it slowly so that she could see today's news-paper and to her surprise she saw her old ballet photograph printed on front page, with a heading in bold letters "Jessica's future historic project—a Great Monument—in progress!" In the article below she found many photos of other Ballet players who had performed earlier in city auditorium with lots of praise. Jessica was amused by this parallel article about her and interestingly, the article mentioned that after 25 years once again for a new creation.

She realized that "Any good work is never forgotten! Politics and politicians have short memory-life, but not the creator."

She saw her 25 years old photos printed along with the news.

But she was not taking up this project, at least not at present. She wanted to work for needy children than to go for this prestigious work.

Socially conscious Jessica had already formed a Trust for physically challenged and abandoned children, regularly visiting "Happy Noble House" and making all efforts to bring them up properly. It was her ambition to see those children to rise in society, and become self-sufficient. She believed in noble ideas. She did not allow separate class rooms for these children. She wanted to be treated at par with normal children that they can freely move in society without having any stigma on their mind. She founded a special workshop for manufacturing wooden body organs like hands, and legs and also wheel chairs. All these articles were provided to various hospitals on charity basis. She purchased old houses to repair them and then sell or donate them to different institutions as the situation arose. This activity made many big organizations and educational Institutes aware of her and have confidence in all her deeds and even her future plans. She was very careful in her plans and their execution. Graph of her popularity was always on rise day by day but she was never overly proud about it. Her humble nature enhanced her personality. She never liked to be surrounded by people and never took an attitude of a pompous benefactor. She wanted these children to take over this institute/trust in future and carry its activities further. She wanted their talent to be utilized for new ideas, future plans or schemes so as to make them self-sufficient and independent.

She had a novel plan to build a three storied building with all facilities. She herself made its architectural design finalized the contractor but she preferred to use all her children to make it possible. She assigned part time tasks for older boys like from making foundation, carpentry work, carrying of cement and mixing sand, watering etc. This exercise would delay the construction but her purpose behind it was to make craftsmen, engineers, masons and contractors out of these children. She wanted none of them to spread his or her hands or beg for money.

Jessica had full confidence in herself and in her mission and in these children.

Many were from villages and were aware of their needs. She was running a Mess in the same compound for them to have full meals, lunch, break-fast with milk as required by each one. Most of these requirements were received from the villages. She purchased hundreds of Acre—hectors—land with Farm houses. Well grown boys of 16-18 years of age were asked to cultivate land. For this she brought lighter weight tractors from Sweden on trial basis and found them worth. Boys could operate them easily so she ordered for some more. Her fleet of tractors became news all over. Farmers from Holland came to see to these modern farming techniques which she had learnt from various magazines right from storage of seeds and their preservation. Ploughs of various sizes, storages, watering pump-sets, siphon systems. She had learnt many tips from her father who was a master in farming. This helped her to teach to all her students initially.

Her paddy crops started to fetch good money. Vegetables and dairy products brought in cash. Cow stable with all modern amenities brought stable economy to make her "Happy Noble House", on sound footings. Her well managed, nicely arranged warehouses were erected near the cottages of her students. One storehouse was reserved for farm accessories and small work-shop where small pumps and tractors be repaired including oil engines. Also at one end coal, wooden bits could be stored for winter season to be used as fuel. One part of store house was partitioned with brick wall for storing fertilizers and pesticides abundantly filled in various bays and third one bigger size for grain-stock like wheat, barley, maize and oil seeds. Some of her students keeping regular account stocks of each of one and see that rats do not grow up, no mosquito, lizards or any other creature spoiling grain stock. Regular pesticides spray was given. Every week end full truck load of grains use to go to market for auction and rest kept for her "Happy Home".

Once in a week she use to visit her farm house to check proper storages, working of farm machineries, condition of tractor its maintenance, oil storages. Also use to check environment is clean, cottages are kept neat and tidy up to mark, curtains and windows panes are cleaned, cloths, bed-sheets, pillow-covers are regularly cleaned, utensils are neat and washed properly, common mess is neatly swept and painted regularly, Kitchen widow panes are not dusty or no fungus around washing bin and bath-rooms. She often stressed personnel hygiene as preventive measures to keep diseases away.

Minimum medicines and antiseptics are always available in common hall where student use to relax.

That day Jessica wanted to go through her farm. Asked her assistant to bring a horse from stable and rode herself through. She found two of students not reported. She was informed that one of them went to his village to help some of his distant relatives who never looked after him at his early days. Another fall in love and went to her house. It was also learnt that he is going to marry her and settled in same village to look after their property.

She thought, "Yes, they are grown up now and would like to marry."

"Okay, no problem, if everything is acceptable to each other and parents too agreed then tell him to carry on—go ahead with tie up. It is even good for me that some one is getting settled." said Jessica.

Now most of these boys are going to be grown up to become independent and can take up responsibilities of their families.

One more idea came to her mind. She immediately asked her assistant to find a new location nearby where new township or village can be developed. Sooner or later these boys will be getting married and another needy will be entering. Why not settle all those who worked and learnt about farming, cultivation and all about agriculture technique? If they want to be independent let them settle in the township which may be built for them as well as others who are in search of house. She asked her assistant to show her a land which can be developed as new township with initially 100-150 cottages and 25 will be for our students who are now farmers. These cottages can be given on ownership or rental basis. Some rows can be built up to sell groceries, vegetables, milk or any other required material as general-stores. Her assistant was astonished but had no other option but to search for land.

In her next visit she approved one big plot of about 50 acre by the river. Plot was hardly 3-4 Kms away from her own farm. She surveyed it to make a road from her farm to this plot and then to main road. Neatly planned for water drainages, storm-water drainages if river over floods, a dumping ground for garbage, small school and a market. Standing on this ground she asked to bring at least 20 workers from town or villages near by to make coarse road from main road to new plot. After instructing she straight went to her office with details of plot. She worked late night to have approx. cost to be incurred and found out that it required huge amount for purchasing land and developing the village. She was fully aware that this village will turn into big town as main road was nearby. Also all her boys will settle with their families and can earn from different trades apart from farming. This second view gave her a motion to build this project within one year time. This difficult task she wanted to be a reality and was prepared to go to any length to achieve it. Next day morning she called up for surveyor to go to the site and be ready with plots blue print. Meanwhile engineers were given a plan of 50 Acre village which could be a town in future. Plan was extended to built up more than 200 houses with market yard, school; water-storages, piping, drainages, garbage ground-roads and all that.

When all plans were finalized, a proposal was given to the Urban Bank asking for a million-dollar of loan to develop this housing near the city. Bank management called them after 15 days as their budget was to be sanctioned by board numbers. It was heard that there was great hue and cry among board members regarding sanctioning of this loan for the new township which was directly going to affect their regular traders and builders,

Who were thinking about their own commercial losses. There was one civil contractor who was very well known. He had previously worked for Jessica and was also close to the chairman of the board. He pushed her proposal for sanction. At last the loan was sanctioned after 15 days on long term basis.

It was a good news for Jessica. She asked her assistant to take over charge and inform her on day to day basis, about the progress of the project.

Now Jessica was free to take up her prestigious project which would take some months to finalize.

—xxxx—

After finishing her coffee she again looked at her Four Towers—Glazing in Golden letter as "JESSICA—TOWERS".

She should have been proud of it but actually she was not.

It was still morning of the spring and cool breeze kept her relaxed. Jessica slipped to old memories. Her brother had passed high school exam and wanted to join university for graduation. He spoke to his parents— Samuel and Janie. Janie had positive views about his future but Samuel hesitated a bit but did not express it. He was aware of his meager income after all. Working hard in fields and selling milk did not fetch enough money except for living happily. He was aware of Jessica's talent but fell short to meet her needs too. Though she acquired name, but name alone does not create future. Money is required for the needs to be fulfilled. There was still time for summer vacation and then college admission. As usual Samuel went to city for selling vegetables and milk by his horse cart. On return in late afternoon he saw building construction going around the city and progressing every day. He thought of doing extra work to meet the children education expenses. One day while going to town he stopped out of interest at a construction site where work was in progress even at that early morning. He found the workers resting for Tea break or so. Many of them approached and purchased vegetables and milk from him. His entire stock was over within no time. Contractor of this project found Samuel in sound health and carried on discussion about his knowledge of material, asked him to take care of his store of cement bags, Tor-rods, tiles. He was also asked to use his cart to carry purchased items like wooden planks for door and windows and any necessary material. Samuel nodded his head and was happy for this extra. This could bring home enough money for his son's higher education. His wife Jenny thought of taking help from her father Patrick but this could hurt Samuels pride. She touched upon this subject but noted that he was not in favor for any kind of help till his efforts proved futile.

Her father Patrick had adopted a boy named Douglas as his son, when that boy was seven year old, as his parents died in an accident nearby while going back to Paris. They were land owners and they had many good houses but they had lost property at gambling. A few houses with land remained on the out skirt of Paris city. After funeral of Douglas parents, some relatives requested to Patrick to take Douglas's custody. Immediately he agreed and adopted him as his son. Patrick was always worried about Douglas being from a rich family and whether he would be able to adjust to this rural atmosphere and life? This question bothered him.

The next day Patrick took Douglas to Samuel's house. It was afternoon, all were having lunch. When Patrick joined them for lunch without any hesitation, Douglas was surprised. Then Samuel and Jenny asked them to come every day for lunch. This was a sincere and cordial request which they could not refuse. From then on, Douglas lunched with Jack and they played together.

Both attended the same school. Douglas slowly forgot his past. Since his childhood he never enjoyed such brotherly relationship. Both Jack and Douglas were together for fishing, boating, and studying together was their routine. When Jack went to city's university and staying in Hostel it was hard for him to be alone. He soon got attached to some bad student circle. He lost discipline. He started to smoke, drink and playing cards and nearly became addicted. Patrick was unaware of his bad habits. This lead Douglas to go astray and he started selling household article to get money for his addiction. He went to the extent of selling a pony to get money to enjoy with his friends. Once he was riding as on a bet between his friends, he was then on the sharp corner of a hill and slipped in the valley and collided with a tree. He was pulled out by his friends. He fractured his leg and also the spinal bone. After prolonged treatment he recovered with some restrictions. He again took up his studies, but had no interest in studies. Now he used to go to the lake and sit there for hours together. Sometimes he thought of going to school library and read some story books, comics etc. which could develop some interest. Suddenly he developed interest in literature. This was a real relief to Mr. Patrick and also to Samuel's family. He was given counseling to bring him back to normal life. Whenever Jack came home for holidays he used to sit with Douglas and discuss with him many problems he was facing. Now Douglas found new friends in books which took him to a different world.

During these reminiscing Jessica did not feel hot afternoon rays. She had even forgotten to water the flower plants.

She went to her bed room, had some lunch. Then she cleared some papers which were brought today morning by office boy, there after went to rest for a while. She found one envelop from hostel. Yes, it was from her elder brother Jack! He had written about his well-being. He remembered his parents and wrote about them. He also remembered how they worked hard to raise money for his studies. His mother took charge of her husband's work in farms and fields like cutting and washing of vegetable, and stacking them neatly in wooden or card-board crates to carry to the market where Samuel went every day morning. Also how she washed milk cans with hot water every night and filled them with milk before sun rise. How she even cleaned cow stables and then washed the cattle. Getting grass from fields and even grazing cows in fields. Help their farm worker in milking cows in morning and evening in cleaned container to be dispatched in morning. All this laborious work was her love, and dedication towards all family members. This letter had come from a military camp where Jack was serving as a Major in the Army.

One day Jessica asked her father while cooking and helping her mother regarding some part of wooden portion above kitchen which had blackened or was nearly burnt. "Now is the time to replace all wooden planks. Better build entire house in stone and upper floor with bricks. I will help you dad. You have enough experience in construction and you have collected most of the required building material. Then when should we start to do this work father? "Jessica, you are right, everything is available but situation never allows me to take up this work" said father. "True" Jessica nodded in acceptance. Samuel narrated to her—. It so happened Jacky was in the city college; he continued to play soccer and was the team captain. He had won a number of trophies and medals. He was declared as National Champion. Once he went to play hockey but while he was collecting a pass from other player, hockey stick hit his knee cap and he collapsed on the ground. He was unable to stand up. Immediately he was taken to nearby First-Aid room. His grandfather Patrick was in campus on a casual visit to principal's office and could see some boys in hurry. Being a Founder— member of Institute he immediately enquired. "What's happening?" "Sir, Jacky fell down on ground while playing and is unable to walk", one student murmured. Patrick rushed to Jack and took him to hospital where his knee cap was immediately operated upon. Jack was asked to rest at least 3-4 months for full recovery. He recovered within two months and meanwhile attended his classes on wheel-chair. His ambition never kept him away from his goal. He was back with the same spirit on sports—ground astonishing every one.

Jack came across an advertisement for recruitment of cadets in the army. He applied for it and as he was meeting all required qualifications he got selected with flying colors! But Samuel never agreed to his joining the Army. Years ago Samuel's father was in Army and he used to be away for months from his home. Mother could look after Samuel. Only one part that his good pay packet could purchase land which helped family in critical time they faced. Samuel's mother looked after him, but he saw her hardship. Hence he did not want his son to be away from home for long intervals. Samuel wanted both his children to be successful professionals. For this Samuel and his wife Jenny worked extra hours to bring their children to a certain level. Jack understood his father's apprehension and gave up his dream of becoming an army officer. After his graduation he told his father that he would like to go to U.S.A. for his future career.

After evening coffee Jessica went on her 14th floor terrace to water the flower plants, cut unnecessary branches and pluck off yellow leaves. She cleaned entire floor herself. It was like an exercise and relaxation for her. Sun was sliding down to her West from where she could notice "Jessica—Towers" shinning in Golden color. As sun becoming larger and larger, towers looked more and pinker. All four towers were appearing like strong pillars.

She remembered when her brother went to U.S.A., and Douglas met with a serious accident, she had become alone. Then she used to help her mother for domestic work and in the rest of her time she developed a hobby of making small toys, statues, houses out of red clay. She used to take these articles to show to her teacher where all students gathered around her models. She found more interest as even her father showed interest in her craft and guided her further. He used to bring plaster of Paris from market and show her to mix quantity of water to be added and skeleton house to be covered with it before it could get dried as finished house. She filled her house premises with different models, dolls and statues and painted them. Once during a long holiday she made two big statues of Angels, beautifully featured, and presented them to the school. On approval of the teachers they were installed at the entrance of school and neatly covered in clear glass. This was also symbolic to the school name was "Angel school", The Principal also got one water fountain in the shape of a Pink Lotus in middle of compound. Jessica again thought of adding a beautiful lady watering that lotus from a brown round pot to give a natural look to the fountain. The school had a small garden where she placed many clay animals grazing, with small clay hut near. This added attraction created more interest for outsiders and architects came to visit the place on holidays. Thus once again Jessica came in lime-light for her work.

Now it was almost dark, Jessica came down to her drawing room, put the gramophone on to hear her favorite song.

> Come again, come again
> Pretty young days.
> Dancing in home and around
> in the garden
> come again, come again, pretty young days.
> Melodious Flute song from distance
> Knocking down silence
> Charming every one on the way.
> Come again, come again, pretty young days
> In evening birds are swinging and swinging.
> Singing on trees
> Cow with calf cheering with charm
> Meeting after long.
> It was mother's lap and fathers warm hand
> remembering me again and again.
> Come again, came again, pretty young days.

—xxxx—

Some people arrived at her gate. As she could not avoid them, she asked her kitchen boy to serve them with tea and snacks. They were asked to sit in waiting room till she prepared to meet them.

Meanwhile she dressed up in evening dress with a light make up, and went to meet her visitors. One grey-haired old person led the team. He introduced himself as a president of some company. He had come with his colleagues.

He said, "Madam, we all respect you as a successful lady and request you to give a lecture about how to go on business activities to lead a happy life without stress. Work for work's sake is okay. All are doing their work satisfactory but everybody wants to lead stress less working-life. Some other executives, supervisors from other faculty also would like to join, including some workers—leaders. There would be about 100 participants madam! Would you accept our request?"

Jessica said, "Yes!! How about a lecture on coming Saturday?" ""Very well, madam, and thank you for the same. You may please come to the college auditorium on that day."

"Fine, I will come,"

The meeting was well organized. People were eager to learn from Jessica, as to "How to be successful in life." Jessica arrived at college premises in the afternoon. The road leading to the college had trees on its both sides. On one there was an oval playground and opposite to it was brown-stone building surrounded by a beautiful garden. That Building was built by her father. One could notice many cars, buses, motor cycles and even bicycles parked out side this auditoriums. There were two halls, adjacent to each other passage; lead by 12' long steps from the entrance. The left side was for badminton court and the other for some indoor games. A part of it was kept for cultural-programmers, like stage drama or lectures. One more adjacent block was for the library with a study hall. Trustees of the institute had allowed these lectures by Jessica with great pleasure.

One day before the lecture, Jessica went straight away after her dinner to her library, which was maintained by herself. She had collected many valuable philosophical and practical books. She went through some books to refresh her knowledge of Philosophy and then of the practical behavior. She was aware of the kind of people from industries, factories as well as from different institutes who would be present to hear her.

On entering the Auditorium, she found even the common space in between two halls packed with people and reporters. Many cameras flashed on her when she entered the hall, which caught her unaware but she realized the situation and her responsibility. She thought that it was really better that late night she went through well known authors, masters in subjects like psychology, stress management, work-management, society obligation etc, and then having made some important notes which she had rehearsal today morning. She was resolved to make a systematic speech.

Now was the time for her to put forth her views backed by practical experience. Though she was not a professional lecturer but her every philosophical or psychological statement was to be followed by her practical and proven views of experience which she had. She did not want to stress on any specific problem and straight away give the solution. Because she knew that every individual had specific capacity to face a certain problem in a certain situation and one shows the way how to solve the same. This is how one has to look at it. Success is nothing but like a "Lotus growing clean and beautiful even in muddy water. So one should not feel any problem as insurmountable." This was what she was to speak."

On the dais, her seat was among the dignitaries like the Mayor, chief of Industries' association, and Industry secretary. She occupied her chair in middle of 4 persons. These speakers spoke on health and environment to cover the main subject. They also spoke on routine chores and various organizational problems.

Now was Jessica's turn. As she got up to speak suddenly there was—pin drop silence in the hall. Organizers too glued to their chairs. She looked around at the audience. There were more than 300 people waiting to listen to her. Even Chief Executives, mayor and all other dignitaries chose to go and seat in front row instead of being on the dais.

Jessica started," Dear friends, all of you are well known figures in the society. Now let us speak a little different than about routine. Let us look around, feel fresh; and understand this nature. Every-body is good, genius and genuine. Every morning is good. Do not feel other side is greener than mine. Coin has other side too, but value remains same. Trust in Yourself. Trust your organization. Have a faith in you and your work. Do not have any competition please. Develop, and maintain skill in your work-product. Show something different from others. Enjoy your work. If you feel you can still do better, go ahead. No one will stop you. Time will prove that hard days are followed by good ones. Crises are to be taken as challenges. This life change has to occur and do occur. It is quite possible that somebody's new invention may suffer your product and business, or your re-search will give boost to others product. This cycle will go on. Today you may feel a particular durable item is costly and prestigious to purchase, tomorrow it may be a common item available everywhere with affordable cost! Somebody stays in big apartment while other may have a small house, but human remains human. He needs meals at two times and morning breakfast. He wants social activities and society to live in. Man-kind never remains alone. Birds fly together, so also fish and animals live with each others. Every individual is with himself, and also with nature and with some kind of activity. Lord—Buddha taught how to change one self. Then there was a king, Asoka in India. He fought bloody wars and won. After going through the battle field, he found thousands of warriors laying dead, injured. Entire war-field was full of red mud, mangled bodies. It was difficult even to walk through. Seeing this misery, Asoka repented and renounced his greed for power. For what did he fight? For land? Or for satisfying his ego, or to subdue his enemy, or to win the war at any cost. Any ambition does not last for long. He felt guilty of his deed and left for the Jungle in repentance. Buddha started mediating, and after many days he was enlightened with the truth. Many people gathered around him and followed his path in the form of Monks, mediating and spreading message of peace!

"So never say "What is that" "I will win at any cost, I must win! I will get it at any cost! No! Never do so. Nothing should be done at any cost. Even in the battle field wounded are hospitalized whether of your side or enemies. Prisoners of war are also taken care because they are human. Tomorrow your close associate may face the same way. Defense personnel are doing their duty because they are employed by Government. Negligence of duty is crime.

As Buddha, Jesus enlightened and worked for a similar cause, so everyone has a little enlightenment that will work towards mankind. It has to work. Every one has to forget past, put curtain over the last night, and then only one can plan for the future and do better. Looking at past is not life. As every rivulet has to go down to another bigger current, ultimately to meet the ocean. Each one then forgets his original source from where it appeared. So forget from where you came, which country, religion, race, which class and so on. Everyone has to reach same destination. There is no other destination.

"So, coming back to our topic of "Achievement at any cost" is not correct. While implementing any new idea one should take care of every small details affecting of human being, and the environment. Every human must be health wise safe, whether directly or indirectly. Also the Environment must remain clean.

"Now let us look at the main personal problems, that of Ego and Greed. The unusual suspect smitten by the sin is a dude who always sings—his own song. Despite any help they received along the way that time. Credit is for that office. Instead thinks personnel achievement toward his own fast track career.

"It is sin—what often goes unrecognized is that people around and especially below, resent the ego, centricity and actually begin to undermine that person's effort in future solution. The choice of acknowledgement of and appreciation for one's peers and subordinates, so they may share in some of the glory, can go a long way to foster ones long term success.

"Now Greed—your too much too soon desire motivates evil while some amount of grid may actually help you, beware of reaching the next level unprepared. Taking this notion to extreme can be self-defeating as core value misguided and life becomes unbalanced in the process. The road to success requires long term approach in all aspects of one's job, and duties. Those focused on quick and short term gains may do well for a moment, but will be ill-prepared to take things to the next level.

"Take Envy—It's Okay to acknowledge others achievements, but lamenting "what should have been yours" can adversely impact your focus on current job tasks.

"It is sin being overly envious of others in work place. It can sabotage your self-esteem, which is a vital characteristic every successful business person shares.

"To—some amount of envy is necessary. Let the accomplishments of others became motivational fuel for your fire in working towards your own success.

"4th is lust—"Grass is always greener" applies more to our work places now than ever before. At the same time, even minor carrots lured by competitors can look huge.

It is a sin to spend time being fixed on what you do not have rather than what you do. It will foster bad attitude and negative overall behave. To solve the "pressure" in office, play big part in who got promoted and who does not. No matter how ambitious, it's prudent to be "present" and make the most out of your current position at this moment in time.

"5th Anger—whether you are at receptionist's desk or at the head of boardroom table, anger damages your reputation, creditability and professionalism. Those prone to angry outbursts rarely get promoted. They are seen as poor leaders who cannot motivate or inspire others.

"It is fine to feel passionately about your job and disagree with others, but learn how to channel those ambitions into actions that will work to your benefit.

"Laziness—It's not cool when you are in 20's in corporate sector—like Railways, mines, marine workshops and all that be indolent and watch others, surpass you—success and authority. The—complacency has no place in workplace, especially for those with high aspirations. Expecting your past successes to carry you forward in the long term is foolish.

"To treat every work day and every project as if your job and your future at large, depends on it.

"More does not always mean better—especially if you are not ready for challenges at hand. The salvation is achieving career success also includes maintaining a life balance. A misplaced design creates a backlash both at home as well as Amit peers.

"Going back—remember "Work is workshop". All religions are equal—ways of devotion—regular life cycle—culture may differ, but motive remains same—Humanitarian—that is religion.

"I have spoken enough for each point giving some Solutions. Many examples can be given for all these point to further analysis and put forward to judge one. Develop a habit of group discussion which sometimes leads to common responsibility. If some one has a fantastic idea then he can go ahead with his own responsibility. This is regarding work. Scientists are never egoistic. They are different, their attitude is different, they believe in team work.

"Now it is late evening. So I conclude my lecture. Think about my views. I wish you all success in your life. Thank you."

The hypnotized audience seating quietly and listening for quite long time suddenly awoke and, acknowledged her speech with a standing ovation and clapping in her honor. Jessica came out of hall waving towards the crowd. Many listeners rushed to shake hand but she straight away boarded her car, and reached home.

The next day while preparing her coffee, she collected the daily news paper, went to her 14th floor terrace, and, sat in the chair. While taking sips of coffee, she could see front pages of all the newspapers were full with her photos. She went through the articles written about her, which contained her speech in detail. The editors drew analogies of her thoughts with the ideas of democracy, and socialism. "Great" she exclaimed. She was happy to know that the report was in the right direction without overly mentioning democracy or socialism "Thank God!" She gave a low sigh.

Today she was to go to her farm, to see her workers, and students and to finalize their dwelling arrangements. After that she wished to go to her village where her wooden house was, and she still expected it to be intact even after heavy rains. Hurriedly she signed important papers and cherubs. Before leaving for her native place she asked her advisor to take her around the plot. She was surprised to see that the said plot was not only nearby, but had a small lake in its surrounding and a green plane nearby. She immediately nodded in approval. Her main reason to go to her home town was to see her grandfather—Patrick and his son, who was also like her brother.

As her village was approaching, she found many new constructions were in progress. Just at the entrance she could see her school and her beautiful sculptures still covered in glass found and intact. She wanted to step in school premises for a while but as her grandfather was sick, and it was already afternoon, she hurried on because she wanted to be with them for sometime. She could see his big house with its upper storey having pointed pyramid shaped roof and its two terraces. As she approached, all old memories gathered in her mind but she controlled herself. She entered the beautiful compound with nice lawn at one end and the other side was covered with white—brown river—sand encircled with beautifully colored, and smooth pebbles which shined in the moon light and glittered in sun.

She parked her car near to his old fashioned car. From here she could see her own wooden house, at a slightly lower level. She found it to be still in better condition.

As she entered grand papa's compound, on hearing her vehicle's sound, Patrick and his son who were in 1st Floor hall, came out, waving to her in great pleasure. As she was missing them since long, she virtually ran, climbed the corridor's steps, went straight to Patrick and embraced him in emotion. Patrick was moved, and his eyes got moist.

Then she went to Douglas to shake his hand. She was surprised to see that he had recovered so soon, and could walk to her inspire of a little limping, smiling confidently while well-coming her. She looked around and could see an arm chair with a side table stacked with magazines and news papers. A small wooden cot was arranged for Patrick, to rest in the afternoon. She noticed things like slippers, socks, shoes, etc just scattered with small bits of paper all around. Before she could speak about these scattered articles, Patrick called the cook and asked Jessica "have some pastry with coffee. Do not go back to city, stay with us till tomorrow evening" she nodded in agreement without a word. Douglas was happy too, and ordered the cook to prepare chicken sandwich and mushroom soup in addition to rice and curry for Jessica. He also asked another servant to fetch fresh apples and berries from the garden. Jessica was happy to see that Douglas did not need the wheel chair anymore, and was taking interest in household activities. Douglas informed her that his one artificial wooden leg fitted by the bone specialist, was actually ordered from her trust, but he kept this as secret since she was busy with some project. Now I am fine and can go around in fields." He said.

After a long time the passers-by could hear some loud talks and laughter from Patrick's house. Patrick said "Jessica, why can't you make frequent visits to us? Now a day we feel lonely. Till your Mummy and Dad were there, we used to have many activities. Now the times are changed. You have given this farm on contract basis to laborers. We do not interfere in their activities. Are you getting your vegetable from this farm or another one which was purchased by you recently.

"Yes grandpa, I am getting from new fields which are being cultivated by my students. They are cultivating not only paddy crops but also some vegetables and in addition, they are taking care of nearly 50 cows which produce milk for dairy and for us." Jessica said.

Patrick said "Very Good, Jessica, that's good economy you have. This means your students, and employees are independent now".

Douglas added "It's lucky that your house could withstand in storm and heavy rains, except the small outhouse, which has been damaged a little."

"I will see it in the evening and arrange some repairs if required. I have a plan to rebuild this house. When dad was alive he had collected most of the required material for it. He had a dream to build the ground floor entirely with brown stones and the floor above with bricks. Unfortunately the sudden death of both Mummy and Dad, it did could not materialize. I want to fulfill their dream at the earliest".

"Any other project in hand now?"

"Yes, grandpa, I have"

Then she narrated her new project in detail—how she had acquired a big land plot for making dwelling for her students, for them to marry and settle down. It would not be compulsory for them but if they wanted, they could to continue and get a plot on rental or lease basis for cultivation independently, upon settling down there but would like to settle there.

She said, "I do not want them to live again like orphans but to become independent. I want to support them till they lead a quality life. Moreover, number of these families will form a small village; even an outsider can purchase these cottages or hire them on rental basis.

There will be small market too for them, need not go to town or city for day to day requirements. This village itself will go with all necessary amenities, infrastructure like roads, water, school, playground, drainages, and garbage dumping ground. These all facilities of this village will turn to represent into small Town. I want to represent this town as Model town; build by people for people.

"Very good, excellent idea—Jessica. You are genius of a daughter of Samuel and Jennifer. They would have been proud of you and utmost happy, seeing you in full career. It was bad that they could not witness this. They worked hard to bring both of you up in life but could not witness your glory. You are still on the verge of progressing further."

"Congrats, child, congrats, keep it up!" Patrick exclaimed.

In evening she asked Patrick whether she could go to her house for a while to have a look."

"No, not now, Jessica! Its getting dark, make it tomorrow morning.'

"OK. Papa" said Jessica.

She got down from 1st floor to stroll around garden. While strolling she could see her house at slope, just a little away and. quite in silence. Once it was so active, plenty of movement along with field workers going around. Parents use to be nearby. Numbers of vegetable baskets filled in and being arranged in store room. Many cows in stable waiting for their calf. Milkmen in hurry with small cans to fill of milk from each of them in the evening. Smell of cooking used to float all over as evening grew darker. Myself and brother going up and down, and shouting around. Now all was in silence. All looked at rest.

Jessica's eye filled up with tears. It was getting darker, and soon would get drowned in the darkness.

Jessica's pretty days were over. Mummy's lap and dad's warm love were protective covers of life. It's all over. She stood in silence for quite some time. Then sat in dark in garden chair quietly till Douglas entered in after distributing wages to the workers. He sat down with her till both were called in for dinner.

As dinner was ready, Jessica herself arranged plates, bowls, water jar, glasses and helped Patrick to his chair. Cook brought food but Jessica took to serve.

After a long time she will have food with a taste; similar to her mothers. She could remember those days when they all used to dine together and Jack used to ask for extra eggs in curry.

While dining with Patrick and Douglas she found Douglas is still innocent and changed lots of his habits. "Tomorrow we both will go to your house, but before entering I will prefer to get it cleaned by some people. Tomorrow morning I will bring two or three persons available from our field. Till then you may wait for me". "O.K." Jessica. Meanwhile Jessica started having a discussion with her grandpa. "Now you should think about this boy. He is capable of taking responsibility. You can think of his marriage now. When I entered today afternoon to your balcony I found number of articles were scattered here and there. Now It requires female touch to organize this home. You can not depend on servant who is paid for their work. Please be serious and reduce most of your responsibilities."

"OK child I will do it."

"What about you Jessica" Douglas. "Yes brother, you know what happened when my marriage date was fixed but God did not allow that to be happen. So wait. Let time come." She looked at Patrick's expression." And more over, career is not the end which I have achieved but there is something more to do and lay the path for others to follow which is in my mind till then please wait." Once again she came back to her discussion "It's really good that you could complete your studies, in spite of all these hurdles. Now grandpa is getting older and you must share his responsibilities. I know now you already began managing fields. Now other things are also required to be done to have this house also to be well maintained well." Again looking at grandpa." This is a time now you should talk to your old friends, and relatives. Something will come out. I can see that this beautiful house requires a good woman to maintain. Age has some limitation". "Yes, child I understand." "Nowadays I am unable to look after even our stable. Many of the horses have been already sold. Once I was holding more than 200 horses & ponies, but not now."

Even after dinner some more discussion took place including old memories. Inspire of all activities Jessica was relaxed. She changed her dress and went to her mother original bed room. She could notice the family photo of her parents and brother & she nicely framed in golden border but covered with dust. She cleaned it and lit a candle, prayed and went to bed.

Next day she got up early in the morning and went to balcony to have a look at her old wooden house which was standing firmly on a slope! Many trees and shrubs were grown around and birds were chirping. She could see clear sky all around with fresh air sweeping through. She could hear some noise of water-mill drawing water from the well. She wanted to go to the garden and then to her house but withheld herself because Douglas was to bring some workers to clean up the area and house.

After morning's tea and break-fast Douglas went to search and picked some workers. Jessica could not wait till his return; she collected the keys and reached her place. She opened the wooden gate which could get only partially opened. She found at left side of gate stones which were piled nicely were scattered. Many of them were covered with fungus. Some bricks were half broken. Most of the plants had gone dry and yellow brown. She stepped up into gallery supported by wooden pillars, opened the lock with some effort from the rusted latch. The wooden door was jammed and rusted at joints, and could be opened only with some more effort. She found wooden door still in good condition though not polished all these years. As she entered drawing room, she could notice the broken dining table, surrounded by some chairs entirely dusty. The kitchens glass panned window was still in good condition and also the kitchens wooden platform. Over that was a wooden bracket for utensils. Many utensils were hanged were dowels, big spoons, aluminum bowls with handle and a cage to arrange for dinning plates, and twin kerosene stoves. She remembered her school days when her mother after hard work in daytime used to burn the stove. Jessica would then help her in all kitchen activities right from cutting vegetables to washing utensils. She was great help to her mother. She could see one wooden cupboard grilled with wire-net to prevent insects from spoiling milk and food items. She used to keep her cake there inside. That corner was completely covered by extra spider net to prevent dusty atmosphere. To the extreme right of kitchen a nicely constructed stair—case was still in sturdy condition where she climbed and reached to immediate hall with attached balcony. She could see front wall lined up with table with mirror and side chair at center. To its left cupboards-one for Mamma, another for daddy to keep their belongings including dresses. Jessica and brother were given two small cupboards to keep dresses, toys and school—bag and books. As she opened gallery door the entire room was filled in with sunlight and fresh air blew inside, suddenly giving it liveliness. In gallery she could see an arm-chair from where one can check entire field's boundary and activities going around. Even now on the side table near the arm chair found two books covered with dust. One was on war and another personnel diary. She gently dusted it and took with her. While doing so she could feel as if her father was seating there. She was moved momentarily. She remembered while studying at the University for Architecture she had come home on her holidays. At that time her father had said, "Jessica. I find too much talent in you. If it is in practice, I am sure you will become a great person. But while on the top, never forget humanity and always help the needy. I also want you to look after your brother Jacky, who looks for quick success. I am afraid any sudden progress and quick results may quickly bring him down too. Give advice to him whenever he is doing wrong."

"O.K. Dad. Do not worry." "Now we are grown up and are sure to take care of you. I will see to it that he is on right track."

Samuel then put his hand on her head and said,

"God bless you Jessica, take care!"

This was last discussion which took place between them. More than 15 years had passed now. But she remembered everything, and was in tears while touching that arm chair. She was aware of her father's ability. Once his left leg was broken while repairing top roof of house and he was in arm-chair for more than a month but he organized all the activities of his field as well as market and his regular construction work at sight, just sitting there!

"Jessica", a sudden shout came from Douglas "I, have brought these four chaps from the field, please give them work. Meanwhile I am taking some visitors to meet daddy. They want to see him."

"OK brother" Jessica.

Jessica distributed the work among those helpers.

She asked them to clean the entire house right from the terrace to the ground floor, and garden. Arranged all stones and good bricks around. Filled up the marshy place with broken bricks and cover with brown sand. Before returning to Patrick's house she opened glass door of wooden cup-board from where she collected many carved wooden pieces showing different animals, fruits and ancient people. One small carved window also was kept at one end of gallery, neatly covered with cloth.

While entering grand—father's gate she found some horses and one cart full of some goods standing at gate. But she went straight way to the bathroom before having break-fast. Douglas too got ready meanwhile to go to the field. Both of them found some discussion was going on about horse trading. While both were having break-fast, Douglas told her what happened while going in field to arrange some workers. These traders were then sitting with dad and asked his identity. Then they wanted to see grand—father and that is how they are here. After some time all got up and dispersed. Grand—Pa joined with Jessica and narrated what happened. These people were traders for various goods and horses too!

This was a group of people who go around to different places for purchasing and selling. Today they saw Douglas on the horse and wanted to know certain things. While discussing they found your brother is very smart and polite. They liked the way he enquired about their need and whether he could help them?

Then they asked as to whose son he is. After hearing his answer they said, "Oh, we want to see your grandfather and discuss with him some proposals". This is the reason that they were here. They also had a proposal for Douglas. The group leader is a land—lord and has a daughter who is eligible for marriage. As you had opened the topic I immediately accepted it. Your brother has accepted it. They may be back here next week. If Douglas agrees then we may accept. "What do you say Jessica", "Very good at least process has been initiated Thank God!" suddenly Jessica relieved, got relaxed: Patrick changed the subject.

"I will give you one room to store all articles you want to retain" Patrick told to Jessica.

"Yes, grandpa." Jessica.

She again went with one servant and collected all the utensils and wooden carved articles before shifting all cupboards, tables, chairs, etc. In fact she wanted to demolish entire house, but thought of retaining it for some time for many reasons in mind. She called up one of her surveyor to have a detailed plan of the house made. Meanwhile she had drawn a perfect sketch of her house except, measurements. She had decided to extend ground floor to give better width, thinking that her brother who was in USA may like to stay here or spend holidays here. She too decided to utilize this house as a central place whenever holidaying in future.

In the evening she was with surveyor giving instructions to make a compound where all the raw materials can be kept before demolishing. A well-constructed outhouse outside the premises will be used as a store room and construction staffs' office. The old staircase being in very good condition should be used after cleaning and polishing. Its retention would always keep her memories alive. All the wooden planks should be removed carefully without breaking and should be stocked on one side, including doors and windows. She said to him, "Now you are in charge of this project including budgeting, purchasing. You may get workers from this village or around in case of need for more. You may not get carpenters easily because they are less in number. So you better try to get one from a nearby village on long term basis. We can give him other work of like pillar carving, windows and any other woodwork as needed by us."

"O.K. Madam", said the supervisor, "If any assistance required you may call me up or my brother who is always available." said Jessica.

Jessica, having evening coffee and the snacks she left to her town villa. While on the way back she saw some construction going on; she stopped over; enquired about whose construction was going on but, could not get the answer, so she got down from her car and found one of her old classmates near the construction site. He was Joy who was earlier staying with his uncle while schooling with her. She greeted him with a smile, asking about his whereabouts and other things. He was happy to see her but got embarrassed before her. He was aware of her days the in school and then in the University where she achieved many rewards and, then had heard about her progress in civil and architectural work. Though Joy was very intelligent but he could not study further after schooling. He had joined one smith-shop with his uncle and worked there for about ten years. Because of recession, that work-shop was closed. Though he was skilled but could not find any job hence he worked in a restaurant and learnt cooking. Jessica knew this. She asked, "For what are you constructing this shed?"

"I am erecting these poles and beams to have a small smithy shop here. Some people have given me some funds, and if I return their loan within a specific period this shop will be mine. I have to pay some interest on this loan. If I fail to do so, then I will have to give them shares of this amount or partnership. I am prepared to work hard and return this amount without much extension of period. I hope I will succeed.'"

. "Yes, you will definitely succeed, in spite of recession because your shop is manageable with less workers and less amount of turn over. But I have a suggestion for you. You should have a small restaurant nearby to provide food to your canteen where the workforce will be coming from some distant villages. See, there is so much traffic on this road and this place is far away from the town. Naturally everyone would prefer to have some snacks, soft drinks or breakfast or dinner over here. Some trucks—drivers may halt here in the night before entering town. This will give you a daily earning so that you need not wait to repay your loan till your project is complete. I would also suggest not go straight way to stock large quantity of raw material for production. This will block your funds. First explore around all bigger smith-shops or component manufacturers who may give you labor contracts for their irregular and odd jobs.

Once work orders are regular you can have surplus stock of raw material and finished products."

"Thank you, Jessica. I was a very good skilled worker but was not aware of this kind of planning. I would have doomed. Its like Godsend help for me that you dropped in as if only for me!"

"No, Joy, I always have same curiosity about what is going around and in what way one can mutually help each other. This always helps in long run. I too have plans to get some special work done from you in the near future which will add to you turnover. Okay Joy, if there is any difficulty do not hesitate to approach me. I have some project for a large housing scheme for my workers and others. So whenever I am on this way, I will drop in." Jessica.

"Thanks, Jessica, now I feel I am having some support for me. I could never have employed some specialist consultant for this project because it is totally unaffordable for me at this time." Joy.

"Do not worry, go ahead, in case anything more is required we will see to it. Okay! Bye Joy. Wish you all the Best".

While on way back to town Jessica was happy that she could give good advice to her classmate. This morning she had told her grandfather about her another project which was to be carried out in agricultural land of some 200 acres. Out of these, 4 to 5 acres of land was useless because it was rocky. She planned to utilize it for storage for grains and a small work shop to repair all agricultural equipment like diesel pumps, tractors, ploughs etc. There would be a good concrete road leading to the warehouse where raw material will be stored. Grain will be collected from farmers by providing them transport like trucks and containers to bring to the site and unload them with fork—lift and stack it in ware—house. The grain will be preserved for long periods without being destroyed by rats, mouse, lizards etc. Each warehouse will be fumigated to avoid cockroaches and insects spoiling the grains and preservatives. Loose grain can be poured from container to the basement of warehouse and with help of bucket elevator it can be taken to the 5th floor and with help of steel screw conveyers to different cement concrete silos. These round or square shape silos are well finished inside to slip grain to down without bridging. Whenever dispatch order is received for wheat, pulses or rice, silo's bottom side opened with small opening to hopper to screw conveyor and conveyed to weighing machine connected to another hopper. After standard weighing, each batch in hopper will pneumatically open a gate, unload weighed grain to gunny bags. Then gunny bags stitched by stitching machine or even by hand as required and conveyed by wooden slat conveyor, will load them in truck for transportation.

Patrick was amazed while hearing her planned project having properly expressed in sequence and said, "From where you learnt all these? Who is your advisor for this kind of technology of storing grain on centralized basis and preserving, dispersing to various places as per order? Jessica?"

Jessica laughed, "Grand Papa, when myself and my college partner while studying for architecture were touring for training with other students we happened to be in Switzerland and Germany and came across some Flour Mills. My Indian partner was Aniket whose father was in Switzerland as Ambassador at that time. He had an interest to go to these mills. Because they too have family's huge agricultural land and wanted to develop warehouses for grains and dairy too on basis of modern technology. While visiting we made certain notes which are useful to me now. This was never predicted by me that one day I may use this for this purpose."

"Anyway, you are organizing so many things at a time, I wonder, how can you manage? But do it carefully. I do not know how your brother is doing in U.S.A., when you have so many opportunities in this country itself?" Patrick said in worry.

Many thoughts had in her mind during her hectic schedule she entered her villa, parked car, found a postman waiting for her. "Madam, Telegraph for you from India, since this is urgent had to come in evening.'" "OK thanks" Jessica signed and kept it on her bed till she finished her wash, changed her dress and went straight for dinner, with telegram in hand. Her servant wondered why madam did not have much curiosity in reading this urgent telegram.

Jessica relaxed in the dinning chair till everything was served. Waited for some time and opened the telegram.

Closed it, cook observed change on her tired face. Her lips moved in smile. She finished her dinner, asked cook to follow to her bed room. Jessica opened her cup-board and removed her recipe book about Indian Dishes. She gave her a list of some of the items to be brought tomorrow morning from grocery shop. She wanted to prepare some sweet dishes. She instructed that she will keep some new curtains and bed sheets, pillow covers and table cloth for change and new flower pots as old ones are almost dirty. Then she personally went to the guest—room looked around and asked her maid to remove the old carpet and put another one which was brought from India. She herself removed some old paintings and placed another from India where her friend Aniket and herself were boating in Kashmir's Dal Lake and took photographs while posing in front of Taj Mahal. Yes, he was Aniket, her classmate who became her boyfriend ultimately while studying for architecture. They had many combined tours of various places along with other students. But visit to India exclusively was made while Aniket family went back there on annual leave from Spain, and she could join them with her parents' permission. While in India both travelled to many famous places in Rajasthan like Udaipur, Jaipur palaces of King. She could guess their greatness, royalty, and various hobbies. Seen those great warrior pictures. Since Aniket's father was Ambassador in Spain from India & he was to visit Bombay, Calcutta and Delhi for official work. Aniket and Jessica too joined him and visited to number of places in Calcutta like botanical garden, British library, Tata Research Centre, then Delhi's-Jantar-Mantar, Red-Fort, Kutub-minar. She was impressed with all that, especially Indian culture, and their freedom fighters' struggle. Among them world known Mahatma-Gandhiji—who was first to give great philosophy of nonviolence, great personality like— Subhash-Chandra bose, Panditji—Nehru. They all were from rich families but still fought against the British. Many saints like Swami Vivekananda, Ramakrishna Paramahans and others. She visited the palace of Baroda's kings as well as Mysore and Gwalior palaces too!. There were many kingdoms in India and all kings were rich, educated and cultured. British commissioned Railway engine but before that kings from Baroda and Kolhapur had laid Rail lines, brought coal engines from England. In fact Dutch, French, Portuguese, English came to India for business purpose by big ships. Once India was one of the richest countries

In ancient days it was Nalanda where many foreigners came to study . . . Indian kings' historical background and social life attracted them. They attracted every one and later stayed back permanently in India. Each foreign empire wanted to be here forever, hence they constructed huge infrastructure for further use and developed it themselves. They too had good religious background. Aniket was from a village town near a city called Kolhapur in Maharashtra. She could see with him some religious places like Pandharpur, Akkalkot, Mahalakmi and Tuljapur Temples where the locals believed that the Goddess stayed there to fulfill wishes of their devotees. She also learnt about saints like Tukaram, Namdev who wrote great philosophy of life even though leading a married life. She was astonished to know that saint called Dnyaneswar wrote the verse-translation of the great Hindu religions book called "Geeta" in his vernacular language for illiterate people and he was only sixteen years old at that time! This impressed Jessica very much. They had limited days to see the Golden Temple in Amritsar, Ajmer and many huge temples in the South. The remaining days left were spent with Aniket's family and there she learnt about the life in a small town where agriculture and dairy-product is main business. She found everyone to be busy since morning till evening. Entire land was covered with sugarcane, wheat and stables of milking cows because of its fertility with plenty of water available. Aniket had one farm house which was newly built up and their ancestors, huge building with 12 to 15 rooms with open terraces and covered balcony. There even was grain storages in the house. This was ancient architectural view, which they called WADA. In little time she also learnt how to make some recipes like spicy brinjol. She also learnt from Aniket's mother other preparation of onion. She wrote down all these recipes. She also learnt how to prepare sweet dishes from milk—cream and sugar. She also wore a sari on two occasions while visiting Mahalaxmi Temple and another in a get together. This is how days passed quickly and she was back to Spain with this family to resume respective work and studies.

Servant entered, and said "Madam, your office Superintendent wants to see you. He had been here this afternoon too! ". "OK send him to the drawing room, I will be there." Jessica.

"Good Evening, Madam, I could have seen you tomorrow morning but do not know your tomorrow's program. So I am here" said Superintendent.

"No, Problem. Tell me the purpose of this urgent visit now" Jessica.

"Madam, some of our shareholders and bankers and previous partners would like to have a meeting in 2-3 days on future planning."

"Okay. It will be tomorrow afternoon. Send messages that I would not be available next week."

She did not explain that her friend Aniket was coming from India, day after tomorrow. She wanted to keep it secret for some time. She again turned to her cupboard and pulled a statue of standing lady in sari in a typical Indian traditional style holding a bronze round pot on her left shoulder and pouring water down below. It was well finished in bronze about 1½ feet height. She called her servant to keep it just near the entrance of the hall on a teak wood table having nicely carved legs.

Next day early in morning she got up from her bed with lot of things to do. She was working like a honeybee. She went with coffee tray on her terrace as usual. Got fresh with her coffee, and looked around. She removed old leaves and dry flowers, cleaned pots, swept the floor and then watered plants and floor. Wiped her hands and legs with her towel. Sat down for a while and took another dose of coffee with biscuits. She was to prepare for today's afternoon meeting and then was to go to market. Before going to office she confirmed that every thing was prepared and well placed including the guest room, drawing room even her hobby cum library room. Only after lunch she could reach office where her office assistants began pouring in. After guiding and clearing her views to everyone, she went to boardroom where most of her invitees and members of project were seated and discussing. After her entrance all stopped their conversations. She wished every one of them looking around.

"Good Afternoon Gentlemen!"

"First let me congratulate all you shareholders, and financers for showing interest in the project. This new township will be like village initially to accommodate some landless farmers who work in others' farms. Their occupancy percentage will be 25% and thereafter we will give all these cottages on rental or ownership basis. This is not a business to earn money or profit making business. You all are here for a social cause. Then you will see this village will turn into a town where you will have a share on your investment like owning a house or a shop. This place I purchased because of its nearness to the main-road leading to big cities. Naturally this area will be in demand. You too will fulfill your dream of having additional house or business. I also let you know that our project is already sanctioned and finances too are received from the government and other institutes".

"Yes Madam, we read in newspapers". Some one shouted from crowd, "Thank you very much, madam, for clearing these official papers. Total how many cottages and dwellings, shops will be built?" Question from a gentleman

"Yes" Jessica said and continued.

"I have a plan with me, but was waiting for additional purchase of land which too is now with me, I will publish all details and budget and period for completion."

"Gentlemen, I will have one more project on the side of this road, may be about 8-10 kilometers away from this. I may declare it only after few months. Any interested institution or financer can join us but only after purchase of suitable land. I am also working out some more details. I have a proposal for a new project. I can brief you the project which is for storages of food grains. For this we will go for modern technique to store food grains in hygienic way and distribute them to the costumer as and when require. This technique will require minimum labour, even for packing and loading to trucks.

Price of lot and selling in market will be owners' responsibility. What we will do—is we will collect your paddy crop or ready grain from your farm with our transport and store in our ware-houses. Storages will be prevented from rain, rats or any insects. Each bag of grain will embossed with your name or brand name so that its easy to know your lot before dispatches are made. This will be at your will with specific rent and other charges."

Audience was stunned for some time for her novel idea. She was aware these people will spread this message which will give increase demand. On that basis size of first phase will depend. There were no questions further. As soon as meeting was over she drove to market. It was almost evening. She went to town's biggest mall to purchase every article for her daily use as well as for her guest, a friend Aniket. She purchased two shirts, Sport shirts, two ties, and pair of socks and two sets of slippers. One for inside house use and another to walk around. Also two sets of bed sheets and pillow cover. In fact Jessica really was so much involved in daily chore that there was hardly any time to look after such purchases. Guest room was just for name's sake as hardly anybody used it. This was also an honor for Aniket! Before dinner she wanted to stack all these articles in cupboard. While doing so she found one photograph with her brother and Dominic who was his friend while studying in college and was also partner for his football team. Both used to decide matches and select players for senior and junior teams. But Dominic was from very rich family having his father's construction business which was flourishing after the 2nd world war. Jessica remembered old days when her brother went to the U.S. for some training and remained there. After working in some major Industry, he settled down there and married Lisa. She was pretty was working with him in her father's industry. Even her brother Ivan too was helping his father. Jacky purchased a house and both were leading normal life. He called his father to join them as mother died because of her sickness. Father Samuel showed him his helplessness to join him in the U.S.A. as he too was sick and did not want to leave his home town and house. He had all his old memories from his childhood and wanted to be with them till his death. After few years Jacky had to leave his father-in-law's slack business and joined Army on short commission as a Junior Officer. While on his annual leave he visited his home town in Spain. As Jessica built up a new house, he got down there. Dominic being his classmate and football partner he used to call him often. Once all three went to Switzerland for holidays as Jessica had never been anywhere for long. This was a long brake for every one. Jessica could enjoy every moment in her own style. Going with them but always minutely observing the crowd in markets, like vegetable vendors, bakery and restaurants, lodge premises with flower plantation, sanctuary of various birds, skiing on the high hills. Dominic came close to her emotionally and photograph was showing close intimacy of every one. Dominic at the centre putting his both arms on their shoulders. After completion of holidays Jack asked Jessica, "Why are you not marrying? If you have decided with some one then let us know?"

"No brother, I do not feel so far. I am having lot many things to do and let me be free from any such obligation. I have to do much for my people, Okay."

"But if you feel I could propose Dominic. He is my good friend. He too once asked me but I had my reservations, because I know your nature and profession. While discussing with Mr. Patrick I heard from him that you have many projects in your hand and you have hardly any time. I am really glad to hear that. You are also rebuilding Dad's Farm house which was his dream. I could not do this as I was always away from home. I will not force you. You complete these all in 2-3 years' time with your efficient organization then you should get tied up" Jack advised her.

"Okay Jack!. Latter I may think about it." Said Jessica.

Jacky, last year, he came along with his wife with their three year old kid from the U.S.A. As usual Dominic visited Jessica's house. Every day they used to go for outing but Jessica could not be always with them except on Sunday's. Jessica's all projects were delayed for some or other reason. Now she will have many projects in her hand including her won house. That was the last wish of her father which also her priority as desired.

It so happened that in one of the Government meeting and another conference she and Dominic were together and some Govt. proposals were to be taken. It looked that specific proposal was shared by Dominic as well as Jessica. Dominic used to always look out for a genius of an architect and Jessica was known to him since long. He asked her to join his project too and she agreed. He was very happy as if he found a jewel in his hand. They used to come together for many occasions even for club ceremonies or parties. He had huge empire built up by his father and Dominic was youngest professional in his organization. After his father's death Dominic was left alone to look after the business and that was how Jessica agreed to help him. In club parties he used to wear gorgeous dresses. His tie used to be made out of snake skin, shoes of tiger skin. On some occasions he behaved arrogantly with other members and had formed a drinking habit. She tolerated all that. While on car racing for 1000 kilometers. he was dominating throughout but at the peak of valley the road was covered with snow.

This was un-noticed by him. His car jumped into valley but it was his luck that even in deep valley he and his car stuck on a tree. Rescue team took two hours to remove him. He was admitted to hospital with number of fractures. It took nearly 6 months for him to recover. In this time Jessica visited him almost every day in beginning and then twice a week to see to his requirements. Dominic asked her to look after his business. She became Chief Executive of his empire. She found most of the prestigious work was done by his father along with some British Architects. She went through their plans, work in progress file. Even in Germany's some huge buildings were constructed which she could see in some photo graphs. She found out names of those old talents and their way of working. After observing this she was wondered how Dominic can handle such huge empire or organization. He was not that sincere enough to do this kind of business. His farther should have thought of all this earlier and could have deputed good executive to help him. She has taken complete responsibility and also deputed two more seniors for her help which may help Dominic even in future. She also found out many project were not being either handled properly or were very slow in progress. It was quite natural when owner does not take proper care. She saw that within 6 months all projects were set in momentum. Even after Dominic's recovery, he wanted her to be with him and she continued. Within 3 years she could complete most of the work and it was in record time. People in city admired her work and trusted her. These 3 years were really hectic for her. In this period her own house, workers, dwelling project got, delayed. But she was very particular and attentive for her trust for training orphans and physically disabled children. She was progressing there and constructed a four storied home for them. She was monitoring day to day work done in her farms, her small workshop and also its requirements and weekly cash required. She was known for her capacity but even though she could not pay proper attention to her newly proposed dwelling and grain storage project.

As Jacky with his wife were paying a visit, Jessica ordered to keep her village house and its beautiful premises clean. She was aware that he would like to show his wife how they sustained their because of his parents hard days and today Jessica given good name after them. Yes Jacky stayed there for 2-3 days. Seen working of their contract workers in their field. He and grandfather and Douglas used to sit together and go through memories of past days. How Douglas survived and became now eligible to take responsibilities. Patrick and he talked about Jessica's marriage. When Dominic was hospitalized and there was no one to look after him except Jessica who not only took care of him but also his organization with efficient way. This impressed Dominic but could not dare to propose for her. In one club party as usual he came with gorgeous gray suit and snake tie was looking toll, and handsome. He was moving in party like a King. She was impressed by this and danced too with him. Then he asked her company to his house for that night but she refused. She was aware of his nature once he decides something he will make it possible. In fact his business survived being old and legend and its well organized systems. Most of the proposals and decisions were made in group. So there was hardly any work for Dominic except checking accounts ledgers. When he proposed her for marriage she accepted though she was aware of his nature thought could be mould as days would pass. Jack asked Jessica "we will visit Italian valley in this spring with Dominic, my wife and you. I hope you will not refuse. Douglas is not available because of grand—pa,s health.

She could not refuse because she too wanted to be with brother's family who were holidaying. Dominic took out his car to drive hill side near Milano city. Snow had just melted. Dominic drove very rough and did not listen in spite of repeated warnings given by Jack. He booked one hotel's cottage but she preferred to take a separate room for herself. Very next day went to city Milano to enjoy their regular parties.

Jessica was aware that Dominic will be hunting a partner to dance. He found beautiful one when on search. Her brother was with his wife where as Jessica was with Jack's baby playing and dancing with her. After enjoying Italian food they reached their cottage. Next day Jack and Dominic went to Jungle which was 35/40 Kms. away. Both stayed there for 3 days. They hunted bears, rabbits and cooked dinner themselves.

They took many drinks. Dominic was fully aware of enjoying his life in full and doing so. Jack was giving company to him as friend, but got little disturbed being proposed for his sister who accepted it. After 3 days outing in jungle returned to cottage with rabbit and asked Jessica to cook it. Both were fully tired and rested for the day. Next day they went to the race course. Again fully drunk. Many big Admirals and rich people used to attend races. He too participated. On first two occasions his horse ranked 2nd and 3rd. On forth time it was so happened that Jockey virtually collapsed with horse. Instead of asking for his injuries he slapped him. This was photographed by cameramen. News reporters could get his name. Next morning while all were at morning breakfast Jessica saw Daily Times News. Showed Dominic slapping horse rider and Jack standing near by. This was slashing to Jessica and her brother's reputation. But Dominic did not show any reaction.

Jacks holidays were over. He left for U.S.A. with his family never again reminding Jessica for marriage with Dominic who had such a dominating nature, full of ego.

Other side Dominic rigorously followed Jessica. Initially she mingled with him as business partner and family friend but finally agreed for this marriage proposal once again made by him. She conveyed this date of marriage to her grandfather and brother which would take place after 4 months. That time most of the work could be over and she would plan for her own project which was left half.

Dominic got interested in his business, personally started looking out for new proposals of Govt. Tenders. Because of firm's name was in a big hit, moreover of Jessica's initiative led many proposals, getting through too! He too initiated interest and worked for extra hours some time even midnight. He was trying to be as efficient as Jessica was! Jessica was habitual to complete her work before time and leave her office too before time. She was also particular to leave for her home earlier than him. Extra time saved used on paper work of her dwelling proposal and her house renovation. She never gave away such social proposal any time in her busy schedule.

One midnight Dominic was returning home on a lonely road, driving car beyond speed limits, but due to rain slipped dashed on a electric-pole. His car got damaged and his hand and leg got injured. Passing fire brigade brought him to the hospital and waited for a checkup whether any fracture occurred. One day Jessica saw Dominic coming from high way in his race car. He Stopped after seeing her. Told her he would be participating in a country wide race of 700 Kms. drive in hilly area. She immediately opposed strongly. "No Dominic, you haven't recovered fully from your injuries and you know you are very rash driver, with high temper. Your ego would never allow anybody to go ahead of you. Even if your car becomes defective you will not wait or get anybody's help. So I request; you not to participate at least this time."

"No, Jessica, I will not listen to you or anybody. I always won and kept my status. This time also I would like to win. My injury is recovered; I do not have any more pain. Please do not restrict me for God's sake". She did not pursue him anymore. Once he decided, it has to happen. One of his friends advised him." Dominic you just recovered. Many youngsters are participating in this winter race. Spring is yet to come in full swing. Snow is yet to melt in jungle side. You would never know where pit holes are on the way. Remember Dominic you are going to drive on hills, your marriage is only a weeks away. This is nothing but your greedy nature; Marshy land is always risky for such race competition."

"Damn it! I can do even that, no body can prevent me. I am daily practicing in that area. This exercise keeps me physically fit. I have reduced my weight too." Finally he prepared for race.

A day before Jessica went to Dominic's house. She wanted to wish him for his championship. She said, "Once you have taken decision I will not prevent you. But now you are getting married with me and will have some responsibilities. Winning is easy for you in race but once family life begins you will have other places to win. No more race after this." "Okay. Dear. This is last race of my life!"

She smiled; wished him smilingly and waved at him while leaving his house. She met a day before because she knew all participants will be busy in checking their vehicles (cars), checking theirs physical fitness by doctors.

Next day before race stared all friends came to wish their friends. Everyone overwhelmed with sheer number of people who had came to watch the car race. Jessica and her office staff too came to see him and wished him. Dominic also waved his hand to all others and Jessica.

Flag waved and within seconds all disappeared on time.

During two and half hours, news flashed, Dominic was far ahead in the race. After 30 minutes, again Dominic record time was noted and announced. While driving Dominic found three interconnected roads. He choose left one which led to the valley after sharp turn and then upward gradation. This made his engine overheated. He had no other choice but to stop and check it but could not find anything. He waited for a while looked here and there but no body was near by. Still no trace of other cars. He understood though he was far ahead of race but he was on a wrong road. He decided to go by short route to join main road. He pushed button to start and suddenly car jumped and thrown in deep valley; nearly 3000 ft. below passing over all trees. Here everyone was amazed how drivers whiz past on the tracks and reached to the finishing point. Here at the end of race every one was waiting for Dominic to come. Even his co racers thought Dominic would win. They would be placed in 2nd, 3rd or 4th as winner. When next competitor reached to destination everybody congratulated him. He was surprised to hear that he won that race and declared number one. That's when Dominic was missed. Everywhere spectators were surprised. Search Rescue teams posted at various places scanned the race path. Even Helicopter could not trace any whereabouts till late night. News spread all over. Jessica had a severe shock but could control as she was aware of his ability and was on phone continuously getting search progress. Next day morning helicopter could snap and located his car in burnt condition. Rescue team took nearly 4-5 hrs to reach to the spot and could get only dead body.

Patrick, Douglas and Jessica went to the spot to see how that could have happened. She seen his dead body, took his right hand by which he waved at her last. Before that he uttered. "This is last race of my life." and it was true.

Almost a year passed, she completed all projects in hand and decided to make a trust. Let some one of distant relatives of Dominic be a trustee of this empire. But they could not find any body. Even no one came forward to claim. She got consent to handover some property to the hospital trust and talked to Mr. Patrick and her brother. She consulted her colleagues and got consent for her brother as trustee. People accepted as Jack was closest friend of Dominic. Even Jack too agreed to shift from U.S.A. to Spain. He too had given his business to his brother in law which was prospering. He even left his chairmanship and president ship of many organizations but promised to visit twice a year to guide them. But Jack's family initially remained behind till her father was alive. So Jacks on and off visits were there in U.S.A. Jessica had to be in control of Dominic's business for some time. This was affecting her own projects which were to be initiated by her. She was embarrassed as her share holders were repeatedly asking for work progress made so far.

She kept that photograph in sorrow in her drawing room and instead of further clearing the guest room she went to her bed room. Last 4-5 years she experienced many ups and down. What kept her going busy throughout was a mystery for her. She was preaching others but now she required counseling herself. Some help from some one was expected. She went into deep sleep late that night.

Now for Jessica Dominic's chapter was closed. Months passed.

Aniket wrote to her a condolence letter with philosophy of life. He used to write his work progress of his various projects at his home town in South Maharashtra a place in between Sangli and Kolhapur. But they made their residential Bungalow at Sangli. At home town they had very big one storey house connected to their large ancestral land, where many workers working and cultivating the land. Anikets's father was transferred from Swiss and posted in Delhi in Foreign Affairs Dept. But since last two years Aniket was asked to look after their farm and modernize.

Today Aniket will be coming. She sent a message to her office that at least for few days she would not be visiting office. She has to go for new project. Whatever was planned till date had to keep going.

She did not go up in the balcony as usual. She got up late too. She asked her cook to bring coffee to her bedroom. She was in silence for quite some time till breakfast received.

Afternoon she was at home and received another telegram that he had postponed his visit as his father was sick. She got nervous because all preparation was personally done with utmost enthusiasm and he was not visiting. Through correspondence she could know that Aniket's father had a heart attack and was admitted to Delhi's hospital. Aniket joined him there to look after him as no one was available. After his recovery Aniket and father came back to Sangli and took voluntary retirement on doctors advice.

Here in Spain, Jessica got busy with her two projects in addition to renovation of the wooden house. Patrick's son got married to same proposed girl and almost settled. Patrick was free and use to visit Jessica's office and resolve various problems which were lagging behind. On many occasions they travelled together to home town and restarted her suspended work. Ground floor was almost ready in stone. She kept entire view as it was but did some construction for cow stable. She intended to keep kitchenware as it was including place of dinning table, storage and cupboard, though replaced by new one. Patrick could read her mind and helped her in day to day work at her home site. Within 3 months upper floor was ready with all beautiful Italian marble floor and Spanish wall paper with Italian colored glass work at entrance and front wall. Beautifully arranged glossy vase and various pots shinning in dramatically arranged lights. Staircase was kept as it was in the same mode of direction. Upper hall's door and windows were beautifully carved in wood and colored glass pans. Even ventilators above door were framed with glass work. While entering in enclosed terrace one could glanced at slopping cement concrete ceiling with all red tiled roof over it. Grill was casted in flower design and top was covered with wooden railings. When Jessica visited she had a feel of her old house in new design. She asked some one to bring her father's arm chair and side table and arranged that in a same location, with extra chair. Patrick and she sat there for some time in silence. Last week she asked her cook to be here to take care of this house, because she and her brother will be visiting frequently. She planted some Daffodils and Jasmine and other flower trees, including apple trees from her farm. Premises of this home were protected by a stone wall and beautifully designed Iron Gate, painted in silver, golden and black color. She also painted the name board in golden color as "Samuel's Dream House". Beautiful lamps were arranged over it, so that it glowed even in night.

Patrick and she could smell Spanish cabbage and rice fragrance while cooking. She remembered all those days as if sitting with Dad, and mummy preparing food. She also felt as if Jack entered the gate after his play-foot ball in hand along with his Dog. Her eyes were wet in emotion. She felt imaginary when her parents were alive?

As dinner was over she went to her hobby room and rearranged those articles which were collected from various places while studying and even after. She found show case was too small to display all collections. Next day she was to go to her office. On her way back she visited her township project. To her surprise her project had taken critical political turn. Initially she herself and her Civil Engineer had worked efficiently as soon as project was sanctioned and funds were allocated for this purpose.

All the three phases taken at a time as were well planned not only for storing construction material sheds but also for all categories of skilled person and workers to stay inside, as laborers travel here on casual basis from nearby villages. Before project was taken all internal temporary roads were made. For this she purchased excavators, road rollers and cranes. Everybody developed interest including workers, supervisors and engineers. Within a short time all plinths were raised up to 3' height. Jessica ordered additional stock of cement, tort rods, bricks etc. Many trucks were engaged for this. Some big business and political people could not stand with this efficient work which might loose their trading. Moreover Jessica would become important lady in the society and political leaders may loose their identity. They decided secretly to disturb her plan. One of the political leaders uttered. "Does she want to bring socialism to our city?" other said, "No, she wants to be the EMPRESS of this region".

They spied the area. Some of builder's workers and masons got entry in that crew already working there to know their working style. Clever one could see that to divide work forces and promised better salaried job with other agencies. This was how they prepared more than 70-75 skilled people. One dark night all fled away from their barracks with their luggage. As soon as she heard of this workers' split through her supervisor, she rushed to the spot. She understood that there is some motive behind the scene. She asked cement and brick agents to give delivery of this items fast so that at least half of the work could be over with the help of 80 remaining people. Because of this incident she went through ware-house, barracks and construction site. She noticed some of the new skilled worker's faces. Within a week at mid night another 45-50 people fled along with a supervisor. That was a rainy day and some of the mischievous workers removed cement sheet roof of the storeroom where cement bags were stored. That nights heavy rainfall damaged all the cement sacks. Seeing all this, Jessica decided to postpone this project for some time. She asked her assistant to shift the labor from this place to some other project or any other activity. She kept about 10 people to look after this place. Her another supervisor was made in charge during this period and was asked to get all the machinery and equipment like bull-dozer, road—roller, excavator, cranes cleaned and oiled properly and protected with proper tarpaulin cover. She instructed him that if anyone wanted this machine on hire basis then it should be given to him with an operator. That supervisor's name was Leon. He said, "Madam I will operate those machineries. If you permit shall I bring some of labor from nearby villages?" "No, some of the influential personalities would strike us again as they would lose economically, politically because of our humanistic approach. They think they too will have to give dwelling facilities, transport to their workers which will reduce their profit margin. Otherwise also at many places workers unrest is going on. Many good factories, workshops have shut down. They are unable to replace that stricking labor by immigrated one." Jessica. She left for her office. On the way she was saying to herself.'

"All those interested to close down our project would be happy for some time but they do not know that someday the transition would occur and this ambitious project will be restored its grandeur."

She also thought of her grain storage technological project to be shifted near her friend's workshop. That might be developed in Industrial Township in future with all facilities. Every time she passed by that road she noticed her friend's project in progress. Sometimes she stopped by for a cup of coffee and sat there for some time thinking about different issues. Now also she was sitting in the corner of that café. Joy's supervisor noticed her while leaving cafeteria. He informed Joy came nearly running to her. He enquired about her new township work progress. She laughed and said, "Joy, this project was for the people by the people with good intention but some influential people do not want it to continue hence they sabotaged it. Its okay I have another project where there won't be any objection, because it will help everyone. I will be having go down for storing grain. We will not only be collecting grain from various places and prevent it from spoiling but also work for distributing it. For this I want your help. "Oh yes tell me, Madam. I will do best possible for you." Said Joy, "I am shifting that project from that location to a spot nearby yours, but for that land needs to be acquired. I will require at least 15 Acres." Jessica.

"Yes, I have constructed this work-shop and café on my own land this is my uncle's land. You know he has no son. I am the only heir. Hence he has given me this plot. Across this road you will get as much as land you want that also belongs to us." Joy.

"Done" Jessica,

"Do you know where my township project was in progress, the entire area was under cultural reformation? Even after 20 years of the 2nd World War, farmers, villagers are getting subsidy. This is also a cause of villagers' resentment. Is this area is also with such facilities?" Jessica asked,

"No, this is a free hold land and your idea would work". Joy.

Jessica had a sigh of relief. She immediately said "I will send surveyor with a plan and within few days money could be arranged for purchase of this land. This will also benefit you to extend your workshop and its automation."

Joy was very happy as he would be having workshop ownership as well as could bring more automatic hammers and electrical furnaces within short period. He could do good progress with proper lay outs, roads, storm water drainages. Most of the plinth was built up by him till date.

One day she could notice too many activities at Joy's factory. Heavy mobilization of vehicles, three wheelers and workers for unloading raw materials. Noise of loading and unloading of metals could be heard. That afternoon she could see smoke from chimney as being from coal fired furnaces as they were lit up. She immediately approached Joy and congratulated. He too bowed down with real joyful way and thanked her and directions given by her. She also told him that as soon as her project would be completed, he would get lot of work from her. She would be owner of fleet of trucks and containers to carry goods. He could repair or make vehicle parts. Also bucket conveyors and their rollers, sprockets, bin activators could be manufactured. "So proceed. I wish you all the best." Jessica,

"Thanks once again Madam" Joy.

Then she left for her own house in village where she was intent to make some changes. As she entered through Iron Gate painted letters in golden color, black background of granite stone.

"Samuel's Dream House". She immediately thought of decorating the dining table and keep everything as she thought. Her father and even mother wanted to replace old dining table but could not do so. She and mother together devoted for their home and kitchen. Cooking food and inviting sometimes friends, her grand father and his son over dinner or lunch. For them cooking was like a passion, so both made sure to try something new and have some guests to taste it over. She was a firm believer of having dinning together to stay together that gives feel of a beautiful home. That reflected the family and all personalities residing in the family. She feels that have been successful in creating a happy inviting ambience. But today she stood near old dining table quietly and lonely. Then she thought to bring all articles, including her clothes, bed-covers, extra-pillows and woolen blankets and kept in two or three wardrobes in upper central hall. Any extra furniture's and book shelf in that hall was mostly of wood and has dark brown in color. She had a habit of collecting small articles from various places she visited as her souvenirs memories kept in glass cup-boards. She also loved lamps and illumination that gives peace of mind. She collected various samples from various places and put all on walls and ceiling to give warm and close atmosphere of "Dream House". She also turned extended portion of house in guest room, and made sure that there was no inconvenience to the guest. Guest room also acts as bed-room and makes life very easy. Today no one was with her except her grandfather who was next to her but she thought of future. Her brother and his family would come over here to stay where she too could join them at every week end. This would give her relief from all day to day chores. This Dream Home could be a holiday home for her. Large balcony enclosed with glass windows all around. She arranged two more arm chairs by the side of her fathers arm chair,. She thought to purchase many other chairs, tea table and carom board to play at leisure.

From her balcony she could observe the field workers were coming near the well. There was large cement water tank built. Always full of water in it with many taps connected. That was for duel purpose. One where buffalos and cow could drink water from that tank and other for all workers to wash themselves after work was over. Sun was almost on the Western horizon. She could see her cook was entering inside through the gate with basket of vegetables as if she was aware Jessica was going to stay back for the day. Her grandpa went out with his family members to son-in-law's place for 3-4 days. Jessica asked cook to make some tomato soup for her and went in garden for a stroll. She found many plants were well grown. Daffodils and Jasmine, Ice flowers, were blooming. She sat in garden chair till she could smell the fragrance from the kitchen. She went through the feel of many sentimental moments till she went to bed!

Aniket and Jessica were fast friends since they joined the architect faculty. Aniket's father was an ambassador in that country and they resided in the same city. She often visited his house. Aniket parents were kind and treated her as a daughter. Friendship went on growing. Even Aniket visited to her village farm house. He enjoyed that life and it was missed by him after leaving his village near Kolhapur in India. He found here too farmers worked hard and fully devoted to produce grains, vegetables and fruits. Only difference was that here in this country people found more modernized and less dependant on man power. Modern technique of cultivation gave them more product output. Aniket and Jessica were habitual to go to apple garden and eat as much fruits as they could of various varieties. Even once Anikets parents visited Jessica's house and Patrick who had given good treat to them in their honor.

Both did not know how those three years passed. As fourth year began all were happy and started behaving like big professionals and as senior students. As the days were progressing each one of them were thinking of their golden days and that college life would be over soon. Each one of them were trying to be as close as possible to each other. Final year students were always given preference over others. It was the Annual Gathering before the final examination. Many events including drama, mimicry, and magic shows songs were conducted. Lots of enjoyment could be seen all over.

Next day dinner party was arranged only for final year's students. Prior to that one ballet show was on card. In all, nine students were selected. Jessica's name was on the top but Aniket did not wanted to be a participant. This Time he wanted to be a part of the audience. All other students were surprised. Jessica's and Aniket duel was famous throughout the college. They were always together, whether in the garden, cafeteria or class room verandah. Everyone thought that they would marry. Some even thought that they were already in relation. But it was true that every one was aware that both had pure friendship. They always kept distance with decent behavior which every one appreciated and respected them for that: It was real example of friendship.

That evening every one came to be a part of that last days function. In spite of going in the auditorium everyone was lingering in the garden, meeting, embracing each other. Every one of them with their most preserved occasional dresses. Because of ballet-show Jessica too wore gorgeous white designed frock with high hill shoes.

She was looking like a queen with rosy chicks and long silky brown heir. After announcement, all slowly entered the hall. Many sensitive ones were also seen nervous as they were from distant towns. Principal, hon. Students secretary and some members were on dais. Every one of them were in sensitive, could deliver brief and sweet memories. Entire auditorium gone quite over it. It was only the next dance programmed to bring students back to cordial atmosphere. Before curtain was taken off, drum beats were sounded for some time. Suddenly curtain was raised. One by one all dancers came rocking on beats. As Jessica entered in her beautiful gorgeous dress every body clapped. Beats went on progress, snick, sharp turn, and round about stretching her arms and legs with rhythm made entire audience clap. Many stood up as dancing groups too were rolling on floor. All were in pair except Jessica who was having her solo in midst of them and was the matter of attraction. More than hour passed, every one dancing on stage was loosing slowly their activeness but Jessica went on tirelessly on floor. It was as if event of the year! At last it was over. Everyone went to green room to change their dress. Every one of them from that group got down through the steps near by stage but Jessica did not. Aniket went to find out that where she must be. In which green room? Suddenly some crisping sound heard. He looked in, found that her trainer cum choreographer was forcibly tried to kiss her and she was avoiding him not allowing him to get into embraced situation. She does not wanted to be a talk of the town or her itself at that gathering. In doing so her frock got torn near shoulder. Aniket could not hold back himself any more as trainer tried to over—power her. He went straight in side and put on blow to his face which shocked him. He never thought anybody was nearby. He beat him till he started bleeding profusely. After protecting her from him he told that trainer to disappear from that seen otherwise he would be handed over to police. He quietly went away from the back door. Jessica changed her dress and went to auditorium as if nothing happened to add further publicity.

Exams were over. Both Aniket and Jessica went for an exhibition where many reputed organizations participated displaying various projects they had completed or in progress and displaying with photographs. Even table models they created. Appreciation and compliment letters displayed on their boards. While going through different stalls they found an advertisement for architects for various vacancies to be filed in. Jessica and Aniket were enrolled and asked to join immediately. Both were given one specific site. They were given a surveyor's maps and rough layouts for the area to be built. Both went to the location which was in another country. This firm bagged contract being creative. They wanted some new input than usual standard model. It was Amsterdam where Jessica and Aniket were to report. Aniket was used to stay in hostel since last year as his father transferred to Delhi prior to his retirement whereas for Jessica it was new experience to be away from parents at least for six months till project entirely organized and initial progress made. Both were also one way happy to be away where their first ever career was to be kick started. For this they traveled to Amsterdam which was quite away from Spain.

Long tiring journey by air to this place, both suddenly felt fresh as the city was approaching. City seemed to be in silence and quite. No heavy traffic even in busy morning hours. Beautifully laid out roads. Both sides of roads lined up with trees, neatly arranged at specific distance. All huge but well built up buildings at both end keeping pretty goods distance from each other and marginally equidistance from road. Everywhere wooden benches were installed to give garden look. Road traffic was marginal that too most of them seen traveling on bicycles. No pollution anywhere. This green city had wonderful look of world class environment. They were asked to be at specific place in that city apartment which was on hire. They could see some of the staff was also employed there. They noticed neat and clean common hall at entrance. They were allotted two different rooms. For Jessica, some choice was given, if she wanted to be with some lady partner? But she preferred to be alone as lot of work would be there for her from designing stage. Partner may get disturbed if she works late night even in her room. There was a common mess where one can give prior order for dinner at the time of morning breakfast. A wash and green tea later both went to mall for small purchases for day to day need. "How natural environment this city could manage to maintain, I do not find any small bit of paper on the road. We will match our design to suit this. Tomorrow we will visit site and inspect its surrounding and accordingly we should plan." Jessica told.

Immediately Aniket replied." Yes, you are right. Now I have some thing in mind. We have seen some monuments in France and also in India near Taj-Mahal— that was 'Deen Dayal Bagh' and some wooden carving at Rajasthan."

"Yes" Jessica supported him.

'Let me draw rough sketches after sight inspection. After that you can correct it okay"?

"Okay." Jessica replied.

Next day they had been to the place where the plot was in between two huge gray colored buildings. Both buildings were pretty good and were newly built. Environment too was beautiful as both building facing towards a beautiful lake surrounded by roads and garden. Both surprised how our firm could get this contract while so many good architectural views could be witnessed here. This was really a question for both of them. Forgetting all both pulled up paper pads from their kit bags; making different sketches and designs to suit its atmosphere. Finally they both drew an esthetic but artistic and lively sketch which was almost similar to each others! Both in surprise clapped for each other and in pleasure. This design was for new council hall. Presently one of the old castles was converted in council hall. Their Spanish firm was allotted one of the big rooms as office. They also organized to help this Spanish firm from local officials and advise them for commercial and legal help to proceed, including contractors and suppliers list. This was big help. From this office they could connect to their country's Office. Distance between their residence and this castle was hardly 3 to 4 Kms. After to that was the construction site, hence no much difficulty to co-ordinate and communicate to office or site.

Today both came from site to this office sat with different designs they made. They both decided to select the one which was principally common in structure.

Jessica made a sketch which showed wide steps in marble stone leading to a huge hall with two wide entrances through wooden door. That wide pavement had 4 huge pillars of marble. Each pillar had creepers and flowers carved in. Design continued from bottom to top. Both side entrances were wide and rectangular in shape.

Wooden latent was huge above both doors with plenty of flowers and creepers carved in with a lotus in center. At the end, each of latent carved with two Angels welcoming all.

Aniket had almost similar design but front view with half curved joined to the centre porch. Pavement had six hug pillars designed with creepers and different flowers in pink and blue colors in marbles. Top of each pillar, ceiling encircled with different designed bronze discs. Central wooden door entrance was 12' wide and nearly 10' high. To this main entrance, two side entrances each of 8' x10' in sizes were shown. Entrance side frame was carved with number of pink and blue color lotuses and cripples After entrance shown a piller-less hall with half encircled gallery and some offices near the stair-case but outside of hall. Both ends of the building had staircases leading to gallery for spectators and some offices. Hall had many arched shape windows. Back side of that building was covered with green lawn and garden to celebrate special occasion.

Lighting was enormous. Premises entrance was shown with a path leading to council hall equipped with side lamps on garden floor and some of the iron pillar holding helium lamps. Garden lawn behind this hall also had colorful inbuilt lamps inside bushes to give special effects. On comparing both found identical designs created, had enormous laugh and satisfied being in the same wave length. Both went to the site and viewed what can be added. Of course trees and other flower plantation would be part of the council hall. Jessica and Aniket usually would visit this area very often so that his building would be looking lively as if part of environment. Both discussed and finalized that project. Then both went on the bank of lake as usual which was just opposite to it.

This beautiful lake had many regular visitors and children playing around became familiar with Jessica and Aniket. Pensioners thought that this pair as a married couple but got surprised on hearing that they were only friends. Their rich, tall, sporty behavior to each other was the matter of discussion for most of the visitors over there. Both usually preferred to walk from the lake to their residence and discuss how project could be—started. As usual both went to their respective room, took wash and reached the mess for their dinner. Both were handed over a letter which was received from Spain. They were advised to finalize project details within a week's time and hand over all to the Civil Engineer who would be reporting to their office in few days. Meanwhile advance copy of entire design was sent to their company's office. The owner himself reverted back in appreciation and offered them another prestigious project.

Next day Jessica and Aniket short listed the suppliers and contractors list. After consideration of previous work, they handed over the list to the Civil Engineer who would be carrying on the construction work further.

From New York they flew to Brussels and then to Barcelona. This togetherness developed further in a unique friendship. It was more than a relationship and compatibility. This was nothing but the love in paramount. In spite of being authoritarian both were never arbitrary and exercising their power of Art. In this respect both were very sensitive.

As they reached to their town and reported to their office with their task they completed were congratulated by seniors and owner. Their design was accepted by everyone in Armstrong as well as in their home town. That succeeded to get them one more project for which dinner party was arranged in that evening where 40-45 dignitaries including office staff would attend. Aniket being always with his parents was accustomed to such occasions and parties. But for Jessica, that was little embarrassing. "Jessica ! It's nice to be here with you. Last six months we experienced too many hard days." Aniket said to encourage her.

"Yes, I admit, I was wanting to relax and now I will do so. I am charmed to find the warmth and spirit of Italy alive and cooking here. Sensuous curving spaces, fabrics with textures drape the high ceilinged restaurant. Bubbling with joy everywhere." Jessica uttered.

That was a brand new restaurant named Royal Restaurant was located at the centre of the city. Where they were claiming world's best Averse desserts and superb risotto. Violet crème Brule, all in a handcrafted sugar globe. That was a sweet heaven. It's the porcini risotto heady with musky mushroom flavors that comes out tops.

Light music put everyone in panache mood. Party was organized to socialize and show off was a part of it. But Jessica wore simple dress where as Aniket too with suit and bow as was in his normal dress. Many of them prefer to have vodka or white whisky where as Jessica Aniket had some pineapple juice, about an hour before everybody got introduced to each other. This new pair was tall, rich and their decent behavior was a centre of attraction. Their work was made known by the host. At drum beats every one joined the floor for dancing. Each one had either wife or friend or coworker made atmosphere celebrity. Time passed. Last dance was a tap dance. Everyone was quick and charged as it sounds hard from musician. Boss, the owner who was discussing with some one got up after having one more peg of Vodka, tapped Aniket who left

Jessica to his Boss and sat near the table just observing all around. He was not much interested to tap any one or dance with any other lady. As the time passed no one had intention to tap the boss. After some time boss lost his control over himself and his action was abnormal. Anyone could see his misbehavior with Jessica who too got embarrassed and tried to get away from his tight grip of arms. Aniket could see and immediately rushed to the spot and first tapped him but in vein. He was not ready to leave Jessica. Almost all the guests kept guessing but could not do anything. Aniket became red hot and slapped him one after another. Entire situation turned in wild. Aniket removed his arms from Jessica's waist and took her away. Some of the office bearer rushed to stop both of Aniket— Jessica from leaving the hall, and to persuade them to have dinner but both left premises. They never turned again to that firm having such greedy boss.

The other day Aniket met Jessica's parents, in their farm house, where his father-in-law was also there. All discussed the matter in length. Experienced gained by Jessica and Aniket and their devotion towards work was excellent. "Why can't you open your own business where you both can become partners? If Jack would have been here he too could have helped you out. You both are professionals. I will arrange one small office for you both where you start working right from tomorrow. This place was kept by me for office from where farm seeds and required fertilizers can be sold. Now this is no more useful to me. You can take charge of it." Patrick confidently directed to them. Jessica nodded and look towards Aniket who gave his consent.

From very next day new life gave way to their profession. Initially Samuel made some changes to that warehouse cum office and Jessica furnished them as she wanted. Aniket went to various Govt. offices to see any orders they would get. Second World War was over long back but collapsed infrastructures were yet to be taken up for rebuilding which many of them were under planning section. He himself went and saw them and to help out and budget the scheme. Otherwise also less number of architectures and civil contractors were available as all of them were in demand. He could get number of orders which would be enough for another 2 to 3 years. Because of this workload both could manage to plan according to priority that Govt. wanted. School, Hospitals were given priority. It was good task to plan according to priority. It was good to perform independently. Meanwhile because of Jessica's and Aniket work in U.S.A. received recognition and many other enquiries too were started flooded. Every day showed progress. Additional staff like surveyor civil engineers and technicians were added in the group. Jessica found it difficult to travel every day from her town to city and got permission from her parents to stay in city but nearer to office. She hired one block on rental basis. Aniket continued to stay in a hostel. One fine morning their office received a telephonic enquiry whether they would make similar council hall as it was designed by them in Amsterdam, in that town? Jessica & Aniket were absolutely happy. That was the first time one prestigious offer was given. That was a red letter day for both of them. Letter was addressed on Aniket and Jessica's name in combined. Both thought of giving their firm's name as A.J. Architects and consultants. That was inaugurated by small ceremony by Mr. Patrick. Jessica's parents were enormously happy that their daughter had such a good own friend who has ability to pull the situation out of grave. Her parents got completely relaxed. Jack was in the U.S. doing his business successfully. Now Jessica too had winning card with her and could crave for the future. As days passed they located one piece of vacant land surrounded by many big commercial buildings. They enquired and found that the land was to be sold but no buyer for it. Till date 3-4 businessman purchased and sold without any progress, for some or other reason. Jessica, Aniket decided to purchase as it was much below market price. They planned it for future requirement. Decided to have three or four storied building with all facilities including canteen / mess, drawing, design office, legal and administration office to deal with all kinds of problems. As soon as their Town Hall (council Hall) work completed, the work for their own bigger office was taken up. Unfortunately this very time Jessica's mother slipped near the water well and got her backbone fractured. This was a shock to her and father too. Work which was to be taken up by her father for developing his dream house was fragmented. Samuel collected almost all material required for it but now he was virtually broke down. In spite of operation her mother's health deteriorated further. Jessica was regularly helping her mother and father in city hospital. Bringing them lunch, and dinner. Brought many specialists to treat her and help the resident doctors but one night she received a call from hospital that she was no more. It was hard time for Patrick, Samuel and Jessica to be without her. Full month they all went to the graveyard to offer flower and lit candles. It was difficult to control Jessica who could not concentrate on work. Even Aniket had hard time to bear this situation. Though he was away from his home and parents, he never felt lonely. This warm feeling was always with him and never thought of leaving this land. Patrick after his wife's death. Jenifer took care of Patrick never allowing him to be with the past. It was Patrick's life style and large business activities, farms, studs that kept him on. Samuel was another one like son and his grandson Jack and Jessica was to fill up all voids in his life. Months' mass held in church for Jenifer was attended by many people of town and city. This attendance was larger than expected. Jessica asked her father to stay with her and he too agreed but after few months he preferred to be in his village farm house and also with Patrick. She understood his feeling. Mean while Jack and his family came to stay with him for few days. On returning he asked his father to be in U.S.A. with him but he never agreed. He said, "Throughout my life I am in this cottage, kept surviving in all rainy days. Only your grandpa Patrick was with me more than a neighbor after my parents' death who was the sole supporter. Those days passed, I and Jenny worked hard to bring both of you to this position. Now I do not want anything, just to relax till the last day. I will reduce all other work, even though Janie and I had decided to build up this wooden house in stone for which I collected all material. Now I do not have any more interest. I want to stay in this house remembering old memories right from my child hood, marriage, yours and Jessica's childhood and day to day development and growth. That's only left for me. So let me be free from everything. Leave me be alone. Patrick Uncle and Jessica is with me to look after me. Do not worry, you may please proceed. If you feel like coming to home town any time, do so with your family. I wish you best of luck for your undertakings."

Jessica and Jack moved virtually; did not want to disturb him. Jack left for U.S.A. and promised he would be returning soon.

Jessica too was asked to concentrate on work but she was visiting him as and when time was allowed.

Jessica concentrated to complete her office work that was in hand to ease the situation. This would help to co-ordinate all activities from the location including her and Aniket's residence, in the same premises. Meanwhile Aniket bagged two more contracts in the same city for a restaurant with a shopping Centre and another for large sports club house. He used art of carved pitcher, of east Europe and shopping clubs on U.S. pattern with modern amenities. For sports club he was very specific in British style with layout that had huge lawn, library, billiards room, table tennis, lawn tennis courts, badminton courts, auditorium and sports gallery for cricket. It was nice to be with all these facilities and both decided to be life members to relax in evenings occasionally. Work was half done at both fronts and one day Aniket received an express telegram from Delhi's foreign dept. "Aniket—your father is sick and admitted in hospital."

—xxxx—

Early morning another telegram was received by Aniket at his hostel address, "Aniket, your father is serious, admitted in Government Hospital." Aniket with that telegram rushed to Jessica's residence and informed her that by immediate flight he would be leaving for India, as his father was sick and admitted to hospital. She immediately replied "Wait Aniket, I am coming with you for booking and to see you at airport." Jessica got ready and went by car to city's booking office and then went to his hostel. She helped him to fill his baggage with all wears and daily usages like tooth brush, slippers, socks.etc. All other articles she collected and kept in another trunk with many other college books, maps and sculptures. She told him, "Aniket you take only necessary baggage. All other articles can be left it over here; I will shift them to my residence. When you are be back I will hand them over to you. Meanwhile our two separate blocks would be ready as our official residence in office premises." Aniket agreed and vacated hostel room and shifted all others articles to Jessica's block. One more telegram was handed over by office boy as they were about to leave for airport. It was from his sister. "Aniket—, Daddy is sick, he is in Govt.

Hospital for treatment. Meanwhile Mummy who is in Sangli for some work will be back by evening. You may start as early as possible."

Both left for airport for the evening flight. Aniket's mind could be read by her. He was worried for his father's health. Sister was alone with him, mother was yet to reach. Here Jessica was already overloaded with work. Jessica assured him, said, "I gave time bond program to our clients. There is no need to worry about work. Take care of your father. Have a faith. Everything will go well. See that you keep me informed as soon as you reach there." It was sad time but Jessica given hope in amides crises. She waved at her till he disappeared. Instead of leaving the airport she sat on a bench for quite some time. Last six years both were together. They never parted at any time. Even after completion of semester or finals she usually went to his home town in India. Her mother's death and now Aniket departure had moved her. She felt empty. Next day morning she went to office, given some instructions, left to her home town to see her father and grandpa. She was there even for next day. Patrick asked, "Jessica do you want any help, please let me know. I will arrange for you. I can talk to somebody senior or better ask some one from Dominic's firm."

"No, grandpa let me struggle alone, Aniket will come back soon. Whatever we had planned will be over in time. All details and schedules are kept by him on paper, I will follow them." "Okay child as you wish." Grandpapa said.

On 3rd day she received a telegram from Aniket "Jessica, Daddy is out of woods, he had severe heart attack. Thank God, his colleagues admitted him well in time and then informed all of us. He is required to take rest for another two months."

This was happy news for Jessica, replied him "Keep me informed Aniket, I am waiting for your calls".

In spite of heavy bills for telephonic conversations they were in touch with each other regularly. Any problem or clarification was discussed on phone. Aniket though away but could guide her about his plan he made and accordingly Jessica could meet the schedule date of completion.

Aniket's father did not want that he should go to Spain again as he was worried for his daughter's marriage. Even many marriage proposals for Aniket were pending. Therefore he asked Aniket to go to Sangli and take care of their property and one of his non-agriculture plot required to be developed. Anikets father advised to him "Before going for any business at our place understand regional laws, ways of working and system for a year or two". Aniket agreed and informed Jessica accordingly. He also found Jessica had developed full confidence within three months and capable of handling every thing as planned.

Aniket went around his farm and then to city's development department. His idle mind irrigated with many idea's for farm development. But for his father's wish was that Aniket work with some builder to understand local systems. In municipal office he found many well planned projects for city's development. He too got surprised with neat infrastructural work was in progress everywhere. Many of them were in need of architect. Aniket was from a well-known family and his father's position in Government and Aniket himself a 'foreign returned' with many works to his credit was in demand. Many people from construction and building works were ready to offer him hefty salaries. Even some of them wanted to offer partnership which he refused. He accepted a job in construction work, building number of colonies for general public. He did not prefer to work for any prestigious builder where lot of skill and devotion was required. His interest was to understand common people and their dealings.

Projects for 500 colonies, each one with 50 houses were planned. Municipal sanctions, Govt. and public fund allocations, public advances and other activities were witnessed by him. He found processes for collection and distribution of money to contractors and to Govt. officials and engineers or other authorities were sluggish. Projects clearance and distribution of money to contractors was done only after those processes were completed and this resulted in a red tape and delay.

Sanctions were obtained by contractors with politicians' influence and showed as if that was all in public interest. Within a year foundations got ready for nearly 150 colonies and all of a sudden there was shortage of cement. Work was stopped. Workers were laid off. Such a huge work force was unemployed. Many of them had migrated from south of Maharashtra and had to go back. Within few months political leaders arranged specific quota of cement for that work which was unable to complete even first lot of 100 colonies which was planned on paper. During his duty Aniket was asked to visit to specific places only. Accordingly moved from his office to various sites for inspection and supervision. He was supposed to witness stones used for filling and soling. Bricks to be used were properly baked. Cement quality and mixing with river sand in proportion. He understood, except cement warehouse he was taken everywhere for inspection. Some civil engineer was given a separate charge of it. Within six months 1st phase of 100 colonies were ready. One night sudden storm with heavy rain followed due to low atmosphere pressure. It rained continuously for hours in night but in morning everything was cleared. Aniket visited the sites as usual. On the way he found some old mud houses covered with tin sheet got damaged. Many roofs were damaged. On the way he noticed many people left without shelter in that night. He found even many of the houses of these new colonies also collapsed instead of getting 'cured' in rain. It looked like a ruined old town. He tried to search the reason and went to cement ware house. Collected some samples and went to laboratory for analysis. It was pointed out by him the cement was containing ash and lime but difficult to trace on visual inspection. News flashed everywhere. Many enquiries were set up to look into matter. Aniket did not want to be part of it, resigned!. News said, "Aniket exposed cement scam."

Now he decided to go for his own construction company. Interestingly he retained the name 'A.J. Architectures and Consultants'. He informed Jessica too! She too was happy on hearing. As construction field was already booming, Aniket could get a good hold on it. Just before he could launch his company, his father asked him to get married then go for anything he would like to do for his career or profession. Proposed girl was also an architect. He was reluctant to do so as he had Jessica in mind and thought to getting married to her but parents may not like because of differences in society, culture and also relatives' disapproval. For one or other reason he prolonged. Meanwhile his sister got married. His mother asked Aniket's father to go through some good proposals for their son but Aniket refused to do so. When mother was on a trip to a religious place in Hardwar got sick. She was brought to Delhi Hospital with some fever. Without any serious reason she expired within a week. Aniket and his father were shocked of that sudden death. He decided to quit new Government assignment and went to home town as per her last wish which Aniket too agreed.

Aniket's marriage, which was on hold for about a year, got through after his father's health as per his dying wish. Accordingly he wrote at length to Jessica about everything that happened with his family. Earlier Aniket's father too thought of allowing his son to marry with Jessica. Jessica herself was thinking in same way, including her father Samuel. They spoke to each other on few occasions, but it was taken lightly when her mother was alive. Now the situation was different. Here Aniket's father and their huge ancestral property on one end, the other end Jessica's father and her well developed profession at many fronts. How to burn the candle at both ends was the question for each of them. Aniket and Jessica's friendship was well known everywhere when they first meet at ballet dance at very young age and remembered each other throughout that long period. Last almost six years they never left each other. Now to be alone in future was irresistible. In spite of this Jessica too wrote to him. "Aniket its wise decision you have made to marry. We both are professionals, developed to such an extent where there is no going back. Your and my father, both are old, both of them require to be looked after. We are the only hope for them. It's also good for you to have an architecture wife as a life partner. Aniket we are good friends and will remain through out. We keep on writing and help each other to groom our friendship! I wish you best of luck!"

Jack came for holidays and stayed with his father and also few days in Jessica's new house along with his father.

Many times Patrick too used to join them. Patrick asked ; "why you and your friend Dominic are not making some plan to visit a valley in this summer. Let Jessica too join with you. She will also get a change for few days". Though Jessica did not want but because of her fathers insistence she went with them. They all, along with Jacks' wife went to a valley surrounded by beautiful view. Instead of staying in a big hotel decided to be in cottages and enjoyed that simple life. Summer valley got fair look everywhere. Valley was full of youngsters and children enjoying games, boating in a lake, horse riding. Dominic asked Jack "Hire horses for the full day and we all will have a long ride. Let your son be with other children who will have group activities and camp teacher will take care of him." Once again Jessica did not want to ride that too for a entire day. She flatly refused and preferred to be with children who were on holiday camp. After a heavy breakfast all three left for long ride. Jessica waved at them. Just after lunch hour somebody on horse came riding hurriedly and asked area's chief ranger to arrange for a help to remove one of the rider who had slipped in the valley. Jessica worried of Jack and his wife who were new to this place. After some hours in evening they all came to cottage. Dominic was bleeding from his head injury and was unable to walk. Same evening, they all left for town. Dominic admitted to hospital with head injury and fractured right thigh bone. It would take months to recover. Patrick, Jack and Jessica were attending regularly for a week. After that Jack had to leave for U.S.A. along with family. Patrick and Jessica visited Dominic every day in evening. Whatever was required including medicines was provided to him. Fortunately breakfast and meals were arranged by hospital. His managers, executives visited and gave details of work.

Finally doctors advised him. "Dominic, please do not get involved in any discussion or stress yourself for any official matter. Why can't you hand over your responsibility to some one?" "Okay. Doctor, I will do so!"

Dominic looked to Jessica who was also nearby along with Samuel and Patrick. Dominic asked Jessica, "Can you help me and became Chief Executive of my firm. It is quite big but well organized. You can guide them and advise whenever asked for." Then he looked at Patrick and Samuel. Both nodded and looked at Jessica. In return Jessica accepted to be a Chief Executive.

Very next day Jessica attended her new office of her own that was A.J. and distributed responsibilities to every one and then went to Dominic's office. For few days she went through different project work which was completed, to understand the organization. Wrote down some notes and then went through new projects to learn the way they were being handled. Compared it for its deviations from original plans and also the costs of projects and thereafter its completion. Also found out what were the reasons of reduced or increased costs and then the market prices. After going through previous years' reports she found the base of the empire was a system and honest executives. That is why Dominic is survived in this profession even after his father's death. This was the reason why he was scot free from all these worries. She concluded he was interested only in day to day accounts or monthly statement and balance sheet. He never signed anywhere. How it could be? Was he authorized? Or this firm had a trustee?

After a few days of working she experienced that most of the senior executives though were salaried persons but every decision was considered in group. They did not accept egoistic character or approach or egoistic philosophy of dominance. Work may delay but no dictatorship was the principal of this organization. She was happy to work with that colleague as a professional who were devoted to this firm. She learnt much more here which was impossible in other organization. Similar rules she too implemented in her firm about which Aniket always spoke to her.

As soon as Dominic recovered, he organized a party for his office staff, business people, and councilors and other leading people in society. Mr. Patrick and Samuel were given the special honor. Dominic gave a small speech, how he was looked after by many close friends after his father's death. He spoke well about his officers, managers and executives who had kept this empire running every day. Everyone thought they were part of this organization and were devoted. He humbly thanked all of them and confidently spoke," the new comer Jessica was Chief Executive during my absence that you helped to keep the show going. I wish she would continue as a Chief Executive even in future. If she accepts this I will declare it just now." Samuel, Patrick, Jessica looked at each other and Patrick asked her to be with him for everyone's benefit. She nodded and he immediately declared, "From Today Jessica will be in top position of this firm till she wants to be. All rights of the company will be with her." Every one clapped in acceptance.

Everyone thought that was a good lesson to him. Only after this accident Dominic regularly attended the office, visited all departments to encourage everyone, discussing the plans and trying to understand them. He too created unique atmosphere which was already there, and gave silver lining as Jessica did. He never interfered in her working schedules. When Dominic was schooling, most of the time he was on playground with friends. When he came across Jack, he natured the sportsman spirit. Both got addicted to soccer and conducting matches with different schools. After Jack's departure to various jobs abroad, he went to club for playing cards and even drinking with elders. Even after his father's death he attended office as a part time job and in the evening with his companions. It was last accident and Jessica's professional work that gave him will to work. Initially he was found to be working in office not more than 5-6 hours whereas Jessica worked often till midnight. As days passed he realized his responsibility as one of the executive and started working till 8.00 p.m. Usually Jessica was always on schedule, completing her work and leave to her own office. On many occasions they left together to, have dinner outside and then go to their respective homes. Many times he would accompany Jessica to her hometown. She discussed with her father about many subjects and cooking in kitchen whereas he would go to her grandfather's house to meet Douglas and play with him. Dominic once suggested to Patrick for his own proposal for Jessica. While having dinner Patrick broached the subject with Samuel. They thought as Jack and Domnic were fast friend since their childhood, then why Jack never suggested Jessica to get married with Domnic.

Most of the time, they were together for outings. Last time also with same intention he sent Jessica along with them. They decided to ask Jack for this, because Jessica earlier was thinking to be Aniket's life partner but never opened any topic on the subject. Father and grandpa were aware of this but as Aniket already got married Jessica had that option which she could have thought of it. Now a days, most of the time they were together. On one occasion both decided to ask her but she looked to be neutral. Samuel looking at her, "Jessica, however great professional you are you should get married to someone to whom you would choose as a life partner. If you have someone please let us know. We will proceed. She replied "OK give me some time." After a week both went to her office and asked for the same. Keeping aside her work she Okayed but only after three months, after completion of delayed work. Both agreed accordingly and conveyed her consent to Dominic. He was too glad on hearing, but was afraid of asking her directly. Jack too was informed about Jessica's decision. He was aware of Dominic's dominating and arrogant nature, his personnel habits and behavior. As a friend he was good but not acceptable as her life partner. Since his father and grandpa decided and she too agreed meant there might be some change in him; possibly because of last accident.

Jack left U.S.A. for his sister's marriage a week before. He landed and reached his hometown found all were in city hospital. He took Douglas with him and could see his friend Dominic's dead body fully covered with white cloth because of plenty of injury while on car racing. Jessica, Samuel and Patrick, were nearby. Many friends and office staff gathered around to attend his funeral.

Days were passed; lot of gossip among people could be heard. Who would be heading this empire? Whose ownership would finally emerge? Many big builders and Industrialists with political influence wanted to take over the empire but legally it was with Jessica. Marriage would have made her the sole full time owner. Firm's senior staff held a meeting about who this firm would be safe with Jessica as Chief Executive? Many thought of appointing one more senior or promoting one amongst them. Jack's consent was received for next meeting which was arranged by Jessica to decide chief executive position and also additional as joint chief executive. "Jack being a friend of Dominic would work as a Joint Chief of Empire along with Chief Executive, who will be one among seniors. You can choose yourselves. I suggest you choose the senior most in Dominic's father's regime but you have freedom to decide anyone within a week. As soon as you decide I would like to resign. This is my decision. See that company is not affected because of this incident, now, or even in future." Jessica declared.

All kept gazing. Legally she was allowed to select her successor or even the president of this empire if there was no legal heir.

As week was passed, one of the oldest senior people of the company Mr. David was unanimous found the choice of all committee members to whom Jessica handed over the charge. "Mr. David. from today you are in charge of this unit as Chief Executive and Mr. Jack who was closely associated with Dominic is a joint owner and caretaker but in the position of chief executive. All finances and final deeds will be signed by both of you. I wish both of you a success!"

As meeting was over Jack told Jessica." I am still an U.S.A. resident. I will require some time to reschedule to work here fulltime. Whatever I established there has to be handed to someone, most probably my brother-in-law before shifting here."

"Okay. You can do so, till then I will ask some one to look after for the time being, with Mr. David's consent."

She called David and told Jacks' problem. David told Jessica, "Madam, I would prefer you to be here till Jack stabilizes. At least some hours in a day or one or two days in a week can help everyone of us." Jessica agreed and left to her apartment. She wrote to Aniket about all incidences. In return Aniket wrote Jessica. "I would like to visit next month. I would like to be with you and your father for few days. I will be coming alone as my wife is not keeping well. "He wrote further to her that he planned to construct a flour mill in his home town including wheat storages and entire conveyor and automatic weighing system. We both will proceed for a visit to Switzerland and Germany to understand this technique. Last time we visited but could not get many details. I would like to collaborate with them. Some renowned company also gave me some design and offer made for machineries which are already working in some of the flour mills there. You may write to them for this."

Jessica pulled out from present grief on receipt of this letter, reviewed her work. Her project of grain storage technique reminded and wanted to learn more about it. She too wanted to know about techniques to be implemented for her grain storage project for which land was acquired. She designed some part of it but while implementing that technique which machineries could be locally manufactured and required to be imported was yet to be decided. This was an opportunity for her and accordingly she wrote to three different machine manufactures.

One day after a month Jessica received a letter from Aniket that his wife was not keeping well because of cancer. Very often he had to take her to Mumbai for various tests and treatment. Doctor advised us to admit her in hospital. So please proceed for proposed visit. Accordingly she went to various places, and negotiated for various clauses. She was very hard on giving profit to any one when her unit itself had many share holders. She also wanted to have 25% reduction in the cost of unit which they ultimately agreed for 20% cost reduction. They also agreed to send erection engineers, but cost of transport would be borne by purchaser.

As soon as Jessica returned to city after that business tour, she held meeting with members and approved the last proposal. All documents were signed. Within 15-20 days all proposals were ready. Machineries were dispatched; technicians' residential places were arranged with all necessary amenities. Electrical Power grids were laid down. Work was efficiently progressed as every thing was pre-planned well in advance. All were waiting for a green signal as many members were already informed on technique of storage system earlier. What ware storing silos? It was explained to every member that silo is storage tank made either in steel sheet fabricated in round shape vessel or in cement concrete. Bottom of each silo would be conical with sliding valve or even bin activator in case of light and fine grain to facilitate flowing down and to avoid bridging. Down below would be automatic weighing machine and auto-sewing machine to stitch each bag. These bags were automatically conveyed, stacked and dispatched.

More than a year passed. Jack got settled with his father in hometown with family. They all used to get together either in new apartment or in Patrick's house. One Saturday afternoon all were together in Samuel's old house. That day Jessica instead of going to office straight went to her village, virtually went running where all were sitting there. All stared at her. Jessica was looking extremely happy, told all those sitting there that she was asked to see chief of city corporation today morning along with their many other directors. They approved and finalized our project of 4 towers, each of one would be of 40 floors. Aniket worked for 60 floors, since last year. Finally they approved only 40 floors for each for those 4 Towers. While sanctioning the plan head of committee asked me that out of 4 towers one would be exclusively for Government service people and its staff. On this basis the plan of so many stories were approved. "If there is any objection then please let us know now. I instantly agreed and signed all papers" She immediately continued, "Today I am going to write to Aniket about this. He too deserves for congratulations~"

All of them seating in the balcony congratulated her. Patrick said "Jessica, I know your adventure is a journey, not a destination. Do not worry whether you win or lose but what is always remembered how you played."

"I, fully agree grandpa, I will never forget."

"Jessica, we have full confidence in you and you have shown results with it."

Patrick continued, "Now listen to me, Today I received a letter from Aniket's father that Aniket would not visit us for few months as his wife expired last week. His father knows Aniket was in contact with you regularly but his next visit would be delayed because he would take some more time to recover from this. Aniket's father asked his son-in-law and daughter to take care of their property for which both agreed. Aniket was to visit Spain and then Germany and Swizz, along with you Jessica! He wants to develop some business there in India. But now has decided to modernize a cattle farm and install a modern dairy for his brother-in-law where Aniket's father too can take interest as a retired person. He too was aware that previously and even now Jessica and Aniket are very close to each other and are the best friends till date. He suggested, we all seniors should make possible for them to be in permanent relationship as life partners. "Let year or two pass; if you agree we will proceed." Samuel informed her; forwarding the letter in Jessica's hand.

Jessica was suddenly changed her happy mood. Every one noticed her mixed feelings on her face. Jessica said, "What ever happened with Aniket was extremely bad, and was unexpected at least for me. But surprisingly his daddy wrote this letter to you, I hope this was not a secret. I will write a condolence letter to him and want to know regarding his future plans. I will wait for his letter!"

"It was our duty to inform you, we still do not know future but Jessica, it is certain that Aniket's father was aware what would happen if Aniket's wife did not recover from cancer. From that time he might be thinking for Aniket's future that is why he wrote to us. But remember if Aniket proposes as per his father's plan do not hesitate to accept it and get married to him. I already discussed this subject with your grandpa and Jack. Now even Douglas got married. He has a nice wife and child too! Jack is getting settled here and unless you to do so I would not be happy. Today I am very happy with your career and way you settled down every one over here." Samuel.

It was late evening that day. Dinner was over but Jessica wanted to be alone. She took a chair in the garden and sat in front of her house for long time before she could go to bed.

Days passed, she wrote to her friend, Aniket, offering her condolences and expressed sorrow. Also asked him to visit here to have some change and try to forget the past.

Nearly after a month she became busy with her new project, recruited engineers, and technicians. Temporary sheds were erected at site including a warehouse for cement and other necessary material. Machineries were hired as work was to be taken all four buildings. Plenty of activities could be seen. Town had this news. Every one was curious to see progress. That would be pride of the town and Jessica's name was on everybody tongue as 'Wonder lady' since long, which got more respect for her. Many of them asked for completion dates and which modern facilities would be provided and all that. Many merchants, business giants, Govt. Officers showed interest to have their residences above 30 floors. Trading shops already initiated booking and paid advances because for them Jessica herself was a guaranty.

Months passed, she received a letter from Aniket, "Jessica, I am sorry for delaying this letter. I received your letter quite some time back. Till date circumstances never allowed me to be there with you to assist in new projects. I am also happy to learn that grain storage system is ready for commission. Quantity of harvest in different region is available and is offered at low price. That is the period to store maximum grain and cereal. Then you will know how much maximum can be stored in silos and also in gunny bags and what quantity can be packed before dispatch. You may get loose cereals in tempos and trailers which will be emptied directly under ground floor. All poured grains also required to be kept away from fungus by giving prescribed treatment. While collecting grains you may get difference in projected and actual quantity is available. This will change value of course. It also depends on market price. You may prefer to store for those who own stock and sell whenever they themselves prefer to do so. You will get rent for storing, preserving and packing. Purchasing and selling directly yourself requires marketing network and huge capital and separate silos. Now you organize on different fronts by dividing in different heads and administration to control. At the end of the year you can compare loss and profit made under these heads and distributes the profit made. Secondly regarding new approved proposals of four towers each of forty stories, there too have separate executive heads and make them responsible. You will be only guiding them and pushing the schedules ahead. Do not directly involve in any execution of activities. That will make you lose concentration on entire project and any bad element can take undue advantage for his/her own interest. I may see you at earliest but not before 6 months till then proceed. I wish you all success. Let me know your progress too, possible I can help you. Take care of your health to keep up on schedule". Letter from Aniket was precious to her in all respect. Earlier his dad wrote to Samuel was an indication which was valuable to her. After understanding the episode she experienced a lovely surge and closeness with him and blushed too to herself. She herself was not within bonds, wrote in return and agreed to accept his advice. She also asked his scheduled visit. Now once again she got extra energy to accomplish any ambitious task.

Today she thought of reorganizing some part of working. She talked to Samuel and Jack if any more help can be introduced? Patrick too asked Jessica, "You are courageous but proceed carefully. I will give you some of the reputed material suppliers. Keep them in parallel with present one. Aniket already cautioned you for this, so follow him. Also you must purchase cement and steel tort rods directly from manufacturer. Hiring of fleet of trucks from two or three transporters is better."

Jack helped her reorganize entire system and also extended his help to have at least one inspection round around, and check each of those activities. He too was also happy to get such leadership in full to prove his preeminence.

Here Jessica got busy with the foreigners for completing and rectifying storage equipments that was supplied by manufacturer. Day and night working could commission the entire system on time for trial basis. It was her good luck that many farmers and traders, merchants lined up near the gate with trucks, container and trailers to feed various cereals for storing. Everybody was appreciating Jessica's thinking which came out of her helping nature to farmers saving from wastages, losses which was in best national interests. Within a month she could set up operation in full swing. News flashed in every news paper on the day it was commissioned. One of the newspapers titled it "Great job by farmer's daughter", Another said "Wonder lady could do this?" Now Jessica's daddy and grandpapa were at peace. They judged her future and nature which would never go down in spite of any hurdle. Only her new township project had a setback because of some selfish people but she was aware of that it would take care of itself.

News paper continued to praise her for many days even after this projects commissioned. Jessica's" selfless services for disables, orphans, training of youngsters for various jobs and farming was noted. The educating needy people should be a lesson for rich and renowned industrialists. She is helping society in many ways. She never enjoyed any social life as such or even looked to be social but worked for it. She was never found in any group or partying with friends even in her young age. She was an Angle for every one of us. Let God help her in all activities."

Many people wrote to her and even suggested many ideas to implement which she kept in mind and replied to all of them.

—xxx—

Aniket called his brother-in-law Anand and his sister to take care of this property on fathers advice. Knowing circumstances he too agreed. Aniket slowly involved him in his civil work. He taught him how to quote for tenders after calculating construction cost. He hinted at suppliers and workers behaviour. How the Govt. people make any process difficult. He made him aware how Indian red tapes in Govt. organization and license system. Aniket and his father wanted to develop agriculture activities and parallel business to produce the milk. He collected various magazines on agriculture which were displaying photographs of dairy-farming and advertising for dairy equipment for processing of milk into powder and also automatic milking machineries. He talked to his father on this subject who suggested to visit the Newzealand. On his advice he went through different sites with his brother-in-law. He visited milk powder processing factory. Even went to different stable, non-toxic grazing area and even cleaning of cow dunk.

As soon as they landed back from the Newzealand, he acquired some more non-agricultural land to develop milk farming. Some senior farmers discussed with Aniket,s father Dinanath and suggested to visit and study the foreign technology of modern Grain storages and Flour Mills in Germany, Switzerland and Israel. Many people stressing to know their modern method of agriculture, like preservations of seeds, cultivation, economical watering system and irrigation, even milk farming. Accordingly Aniket and his brother-law-Anand arranged their 10-12 days tour and booked lodges in Hamburg. He wrote to Jessica his plan and asked her "Jessica ! if you could join at Hamburg along with your brother, would help me also to assist to you. As such you are very busy for those 4 prestigious towers, let your brother administer the storage and farming technique. As soon as your reply is received I will book a separate room for you. You may discuss this program to your Dad and grandfather too!"

Accordingly matter was discussed with Jack who was very happy to go through various mills and modern technique at Israel's agriculture and milk farming. Patrick asked Jessica "Okay, you both can visit to those places but what about Anikets way back to India?"

"I do not know, grand—pa, that is not yet clear to me so far." replied Jessica.

Patrick said "Now you can convey him that he should visit us before returning to India and see whatever projects are completed or on the way of completion".

"Okay,. I will do so, I am sure he will not deny."

As soon as Aniket received confirmation from Jessica and Jack, he booked two rooms in Hotel Plaza which was near to their Hotel Imperial. Aniket and Anand went with Daffodils bouquet to receive them at airport. As both landed and approached the main gate both could see each other from a distant, waving to each others smilingly. As she came close to him, Aniket handed over to her the bouquet of pink daffodils. She remembered similar incident where he offered her daffodil as a winner of a ballet. Tears virtually rolled out of her eyes, her cheeks turned pink, remembered all past. Anand was introduced to Jessica and Jack. He too handed over bouquet to Jack who pleased and thanked to both of them.

Jessica said in grief "Aniket, Thanks for this and calling to join with you and with your brother-in-law. I am sorry to here the sudden departure of your wife. I could understand your feeling!"

"Jessica, yes. It was not sudden, but I made all possible effort to survive her but in vain." Aniket, Sadly expressed.

"Okay,. let us move from here and go to your lodge first. Aniket I would like to hear many things from you, then we will go to Hotel plaza!" Jessica.

All went ; got fresh, waiter brought some snacks and coffee for them but Aniket was not much in the mood to discuss about his personnel problems he faced during that period. But expressed how he was now progressing, his future plans and even how this visit in various countries could help every one of us." Ultimately we are going to build big empire for our people!" Exclaimed Aniket.

Anand and Jack were new to many new Industries of Flour mills, storages, ware—house technique, modern milk farming and making various product from milk like, milk—powder, tone milk, and its preservation. Both took keen interest. Put down some notes on their note-books. Aniket and Jessica were trying to find out what was missed in last visit and what could be modified after reaching to their own unit. They found much similarity of technique, machine design in Germany, Swiss, Italy. They found Germans Machines were sturdier than others.

Italian machineries found to be light and cost wise much cheaper then Germany and Swiss made. Swiss machineries were mean of German and Italy with little more improved and with latest technology but costlier than other. Every manufacturer had speciality to win over another. These purchases were depending on buying affordability of customer.

Before leaving for Israel they all went to Swiss valley. Jack and Anand wanted to enjoy skiing and even participate in competition. "Jack never leaves any chance of sporting. After long time he would enjoy this, but he does not have any practice since long." Jessica.

On that Aniket worriedly said to Anand, "look here Anand, you too are new to this skiing, I do not know how you would play. If any difficulty faced during skiing leave it there and take support of slug and come back."

Immediately Anand replied "Do not worry, I will be safe, I am not playing for any competition or to get name or fame . . . ."

Siren blown and all set off to skied!. Jack as usual was ahead of all of them and of course Anand was almost last of two, but enjoying new experience. Within one hour Anand came back fully exhausted, as he was not having any trick to play. Nearly after about 2 hrs Jack came as a winner and was so happy, raising both sticks up and waving at the crowd. Next day Aniket along with Anand went to Jacks room who was warming himself in bed, do not wanted to go out. Anand too joined him, as he too was tired. Then Aniket alone went to Jessica's room to find out whether she would like to stroll out with him? she agreed. Both went in the park., nearby. and sat there for quite some time with hot coffee observing scenic beauty, from where they could observe clouds fleeing in middle of the mountain, cool breeze all around, dense fog added to that atmosphere made them little shivery. Shivery weather was nothing but prior indication of snow fall and within few minutes snow flakes could be seen freely falling freely flowing and continued to fall. Pine trees were all around, as if stretching their hands to collect snow and cover them—self. Aniket had woolen long over coat. He removed it and put on her shoulder to protect her. While doing so she had deep look into his brown blue eyes. Sprinkling her heart to him. "Aniket, you are doing so much for me, but in fact I never done anything for you." Jessica said in emotion.

Aniket said "Jessica, nothing was done by me. It was my internal spirit that always kept me with you. I remember our days at Amsterdam. Those six months were precious to both of us where we developed in every respect. Our love too bloomed there on the bank of silent lake. I also know that my father some time back spoke to your father. I know what was happening, but could not get out of the situation as somebody was required at my home town to take care of our property and house that I was developing. I am training Anand for that. He has courage to be a sphere head in our activities! Jessica, our love is not like others. We work towards our duties, society which is a long process. If our love is blooming then we would be achieving many objectives of our life which need not be spoken. We are best friend and will remain forever! But our need is to convert the friendship in marriage. It is also agreed by both of our families. Our ties across countries will be best lesson to every individual. Now as soon as Israel's visit is over I will come down to your village and give my consent to your Daddy and Grandpa."

Jessica was aware of this when Aniket gave her bouquet of daffodils which was the first site of his brown blue eyes sparked in her deep emotions. Without expressing she could experienced everything at air-port. Jessica was absolutely happy just at that moment which turned her life as if blooming a lotus in love pond. She embraced him. That surge of emotion killed all her shivering in cold. Additional dose of coffee gave them boost to be free to each other which was never before. Aniket left Jessica in her room. It was still snowy everywhere. He took Anand with him from Jacks room who had enough warming from fire and drinks.

The other day all flew to Israel gone through various farming units, research organizations in agricultural institute and factories manufacturing equipment.

Many of the modern technique were found more economical than us. Aniket ordered some of them on urgent basis and left for Jessica's home land. Jack took them to Patrick's house directly from air port.

It was late evening, Jack, Anand, and Aniket preferred to be in Patrick house, but Jessica preferred to be with her daddy, hence she left with her luggage to her home. Samuel was too happy and affectionately pat her. He could notice big change in her smile and the way she was lightly moving here and there. Douglas came in with dinner for both of them and went back to join others. While dinning she expressed her views on Aniket decision of changing friendship in permanent relation of marriage. Samuel gave deep sigh of relief. He laughed, congratulated her. "Child, I know, if this would have not happened then you would have never got married. All your activities were enough for you to keep busy. Now I am free from all worries as you both agreed to tie a knot."

"Jessica, are you aware that your "Happy Home for children" will be completing ten years day after tomorrow. All trustees and members of this had been here last week. They would like to conduct small ceremony to be held with all students of your institute and their parents. Of course many of them are orphan, and ex—student too!.."

"Yes, dad! I wanted that those trustee members and in charge should lead this ceremony. This is a social work and everyone is part of it. I will definitely going to join. Every week I am regularly visiting and once in a month I live with them for a complete day. Nearly twenty five student though they are disable, orphan or even admitted by their parents in our institution, requires parenting. They are longing for it. Many of them required counseling which is also main roll of this institute. Only by giving artificial organs to disable and two time food was never enough. Practically they have to stand on their own and face this world of challenges. For that, this institute stands!"

"Yes, Jessica, I am aware of all your efforts and devotion towards it. I too know someone should slowly take over this responsibility. Only professional way may not work here but, personnel touch is also required to worm up them."

Next day everybody joined Samuel's home for morning break-fast. Jessica herself prepared slightly spicy suji and omelet. While having tea, Patrick opened topic and talked to Samuel regarding Aniket and Jessica's engagement. That house witnessed free and happy atmosphere, may be after decades. Jessica was seen to be light hearted; as if her childhood returned to her once again. She had no expression of any sort at that moment. Patrick taken a lead, "Aniket ! let us decide for engagement, now we know that you both cannot live without each other. Even your father too of that opinion. Let us have some tentative date for engagement."

"Yes, I would prefer that but let Jessica complete her present project. Meanwhile I will also complete milk farm project and hand over to Anand. It may take about six to seven months for its completion."

"I feel you all should come here for engagement. you can bring your close relatives and friends over here that time, but better to make little early. I am also not keeping well. It is Jessica's view that she wants to get married in India in your traditional way. Possible she read in magazines and also attended some marriages in your town in India. She impressed that lighting of fire and ancient Veda mantra, that priest chants. She showed us some photographs of marriage ceremony. I would also feel let us go in her way. I am of the opinion that now she should live her life in her own way and get settle where ever you both prefer." Samuel spoke while Patrick and Jack too agreed.

Patrick once again asked. "Jessica, what is your and Anikets opinion on this issue?"

Jessica said, "Yes grandpa, let engagement be here regarding marriage—I decided to go Indian way, dressed in traditional sari and Sherwin., We as couple tie the knot according to Vedic customs. In this custom Bride and Groom together arrives at a reception, riding on a four wheeler Horse cart, called baggy with baratis that is participant, would be dancing and cheering along the way. We decided to our vows according to Hindu rites as I am, fascinated by the rich culture and customs."

The other day all four decided to visit various work places at different location and work in progress. Jessica informed Aniket "today we will be visiting all work places, but my Happy Home is kept for day after tomorrow. We will be celebrating there 10th anniversary of this institute. All our house member including dad and grand-pa will be there.

"Absolutely fine." said Aniket and Jack.

Aniket, Jack, Anand, and Jessica prepared to board a car, Douglas came running and joined them. Though he was there all the time but never had opportunity to go through all work of Jessica. Whatever he heard about her work was only through family discussion and people talked about. First they went to her 200 Acre Farm. She explained how those 20 students were trained for cultivating various grains and cereals but also learned manual technique of storing these goods. She further added." I have provided them different ware—houses including storing of fertilizers, and farm equipments. Even I asked them, guided them for erecting cow stable and how to milk them. All milk is consumed by them and children in our Happy Home. Some portion of land is reserved for vegetables and fruits, so no purchases from the market. They keep a log of all sale—purchases and stores materials on day to day basis. All these student together have a dormitory and cottages on the boarder of this farm house. I will show you their combined mess where everyone in turn in group of 3 or 4 students cook the food for everyone. I found they are really enjoy this life."

She continued, "I could observed, many grown up students would like to marry and settle down nearby. They would like to have their own family or to work for others. I have no restrictions for them. They can even work for our farm on wedges after their marriages. For all of such and also for outsiders I planned to develop one village near by which could be turned into township. For that purpose I purchased separate land at the bank of the lake. There are some big influenced politicians and businessman, merchants flushed out my work in the half way for their selfish motto, hence I have to drop that project. I know some or other day this scheme would be materialize itself being in need."

Looking at Jack and Douglas, she said. "I feel, Jack, after few days or so, you will have to complete this work and settle new township as I planned. You can approach higher authority in charge, who have already permitted this project and bank too ready to help".

While going to city she diverted all of them to the site where she acquired land and partly developed foundations, roads, storm water drainages, Trees planted already grown high and given a good environmental look and attracts everyone as added to its future developments. Then they turned to have a look at how they have built up schools, Hospital for city's corporation. Thereafter with Aniket's initiative how they could construct one of the tall building for Hotel with marketing shop within premises. Then, visited sports.—Club with all facilities including beautiful green ground for various outdoor games. Finally they proceeded to go through the four towers,—forty storied building project. She took them all around and explained. "This was prestigious work with various use and purpose where Govt. itself was very much interested for its earliest completion. Therefore whole of my concentration was on these activities. Now a day's Jack too helping me and developed enough interest including Dominic Empire's work." At the end everybody went to her present office which was being started its work when Aniket had to leave for India. It's Jessica who took over and completed.

Now Jessica herself live on its top terrace floor, kept office at ground and 1st floor. Others still kept vacant for Jack or Aniket when they would be here. This earlier planning could ease for Aniket to stay away from Hostel was an idea behind this.

After lunch they stroll all over the city and next day attended their Happy home's 10th Annual Anniversary. Patrick joined along with Samuel and others.

Jessica was on dais along with other Trustees and some members. Jessica called her father and grand-pa to publish a yearly magazine and distribute the prizes. Grand-pa gave a small inaugural speech, praised Jessica and trustees, who worked for the welfare of the society. He praised every one sportily and encouraged for their daily chores. He said, "These student are not disables. They might have faced some or other unfortunate phase of the life that does not mean they are away from main stream of the society. They are part and parcel of the progress of our country. They have inherent quality and intelligent too! I request every one of you to bring out their valuable hidden genes, one can see wonder from them. He pointed out at Jack and Douglas". Look my grandson and my son both were lame but today they are absolutely outstanding, then why other should not be!"

Press reporters and cameraman were doing their job as usual. otherwise also wherever Jessica's public appearance was possible, they were always there.

Jessica was asked to speak for which her students and entire audience were waiting. Her charming tall personality with simple leaving was always remained a matter of discussion. She stood, both deep brown-blue eyes went through the crowd affectionately.

"All my students and their parents, and colleague, who are responsible for today's 10th anniversary are the pillars of this Happy Home. I congratulate all of you. On this occasion I would say some words. On this day I declare, that this Happy Home is renamed as "Golden Dream House" why I added a Golden Word. It's simple but very important feature of everyone's life. You all aware the house I mean Home is initially commissioned to help disable to give them artificial organs with the advice of doctors and orthopedic. By mere giving or operating on limps and arms does not mean we have helped them. I thought of accommodating them in this house, and give those orphan and disable children a shelter with food and cloths. Again here also I thought it's not enough just bringing them under common roof but let them use their talent by working. Therefore I installed work—shop and craft-mans house which can train them on various aspects of practical life. Then I found many children who are not orphan but disable required assistance for necessary recovery to lead a normal life are also admitted. All these children worked, showed more and more interest for making various articles which are purchased by many people. Today we have collected quite a good amount of money from this sell, apart from donations. Today I am giving four uniform to all those students. Two for class-room and two for workshop or vocational training. If you go through the magazine which is distributed to every one of you can make you aware how children are kept busy throughout the day."

She pointed out and said "I can see many parents and even other people are present to witness this occasion. I would suggest few important points.—The major our present society of parents are traditional in their outlook but they want to educate their offspring in modern educational institute. As parents change attitude towards learning in their children., initially I worked hard because I wanted to use optimal blending of old and new. There seems to be confusion and parents often ends up arguing with children with result that children begin to resist education. It is not so much a question of de-learning as a question of self learning. If parent wants to bring about change of attitude towards learning in their children they must prepare themselves to be good counselors. There is a great deal of lack of parental counseling. Another problem is pampering. Parents have great affection for their children and this often leads to pampering them. while affection is good, pampering is bad. Children become easy going and that is worst thing that can happen. They become fussy and refuse to heed advice. They know nothing but their own desires. Harsh realities have no place in their dictionary. It is for this reason that pampered child cannot meet challenges, they have to face in the external world."

I myself initially taught them discipline, then practical work and there after class-room study. I pet them too whenever they do special. My worm palm on their shoulder is enough, in fact that affectionate touch is necessary for everyone.

So Golden means the opportunity for all these children mainly disables who were unfortunate that specific time, but now they have to over ride Godly calamities and rode ahead. This is Golden time in every one's life. These efforts you are putting under the roof of this house to prove or set to achieve dream hence this is a "Golden Dream House" From today this institute will function as a "Golden Dream House".

All participants rose to applaud. Samuel and Patrick stood in wet eyes. That she is a real Jewel which was unearthed by all of us. After few seconds she raised both arm said, "Listen to me. let me tell you we are not God, We are born on this earth to establish relationship for better life and nothing else." As soon as her speech was over,. Cameras flashed all over. Patrick came up on stage and affectionately took her near and pet her. Samuel, Aniket, Jack to followed, said "Yes, you have done it!"

After all these visits, Anand asked Aniket, "What about Grain storages, automatic conveyer system and all that, I am too much interested to look at it. What we have seen was quite large size storages for flour mill."

"Yes, Anand tomorrow before leaving this place, we will be visiting to see that also. Today it is quite late and possibly could have stopped by now." Aniket.

"Yes, we will visit grain storage plant, but I kept it for tomorrow as I have to instruct for some modification in the hoppers and conveying system which we have observed lately in Swiss."

Next day all of them visited various sections of the plant like unloading of loose grain, from trucks and containers. That grain dumped in pit, automatically collected with help of chain of buckets and dropped in various silos. They are again automatically weighted, filled in bags and conveyed down through wooden chutes to load into trucks or to storing places or delivered to customers as per the order.

Aniket pet Jessica said, "You are a gem of a lady who alone could set such a huge project, commissioned and operated successfully. This collection of grains, storages, preservation is national work for society. You are always on look to help with some or other way, whether somebody is with you or not. Many occasion people spoil your project but your determined hope for the future to happen so! I admire you and your courage."

Aniket, Anand left for India, promising would be back within six months along with his dad and others for a engagement with Jessica.

—xxx—

In India a marketing representative from Switzerland, New Zealand and Israel reached before Aniket and Anand could reach to Kolhapur. Aniket was just got in surprise of those smart and efficient marketing representative. All three were given different contract on merit basis. One by one Aniket showed the site where the milk farm will be erected. He shown the permanent sheds he erected for cows and buffalos. He proposed the place for Cold storages where milk would be stored and preserved. Plinth for all those were ready except for installation of machineries to manufacture the milk powder and tone milk.

Those representative advised Aniket to have two separate phases. One phase where the milk collected from outside would be stored and transferred to cold storage. For this 5-6 steel tanks were to be insulated by thermo cool or clothes. Deep freezers operation at—5 to—7^0C temp would be maintained by compressed Freon gas filled in with cooling tower arrangement. From here milk outlet would be unlocked and milk would transported by steel tube to small hopper, under which polythene bags of required volume and weight would be automatically filled in and sealed.

The second part of the phase was to manufacture the milk power. Here also involved deep freezing system. Huge conical round shaped steel vessel jacketed from outside to flow steam inside which produced by water steam boiler that installed. The preserved milk flows inside the vessel, heated by steam, circulated through jacket to form white milk power.

This Powder samples would be send to laboratory to find out various contents like fat, carbohydrates, proteins, vitamins. Powder collected in the Bins are ready for packing in Aluminum tins are sealed, labeled and ready for dispatches but not before being passed through food and Drug department.

Ready Tin Powder containers would be conveyed on belt and filled in cartoon for distribution.

A representative from Israel had to wait for another day. Mean while Aniket and his father and Anand discussed, found various differences on analyzing and classifying in various aspects of technology, consultation and services given thereafter. Next was Israel who was keen to get order for agriculture equipments like dosing pump for spraying pesticides, sprinklers for watering, drip irrigation, using of fertilizers, high-breed-seeds and plough technique. Anand was from farmers family but he wanted to learn all those which would be a long term co-ordination between Israel's firm and Aniket. Anand accepted to go this long way of learning. They also put orders for some urgent equipment with Israel.

Days passed, months passed. All those three parallel activities were in progress where as Aniket concentrated on marketing. Temporary basis he purchased ice factory's idle old machineries and equipments and installed near his farm house with refrigeration system. He got fabricated steel tank and insulted it with cotton and wool. He himself went to various villages nearby Kolhapur and Sangli town to get regular daily milk supply from farmers. He offered fair price for them if get hundreds of liters from nearest villages. Many of them agreed. Hired small steel road tankers which could reach to various villages early morning and collect milk from each of them. Initially though promised by villagers he could get only half of quota which was not economical for processing or even for manual packing. He then approached farmers co-operative bank and asked for loan to purchase some buffalos and cows which they immediately agreed. It was good that he already had erected number of shelters for them. Fodder too was available for it but again manpower was a problem. He talked to various poor people who could take cow and feed them but milk produced would be given to his dairy for which they would be given substantial labor charges. They were very happy to go ahead with this scheme. Within three months systematic schedule was launched. This was a successful business venture and within few days milk producers enrolment soared. He crossed calculated target of collection of milk. Now he thought of some selfish people may spoil this co-operative work. For precautionary measure he again purchased more milking cows for himself and kept them in his stable. This progress was noticed by Swiss and New Zealand engineers and asked Aniket to provide more technician to match his target. Most of the machineries and equipments were arrived. Necessary inspection was carried out together. Priority was given to refrigeration plant. As soon as cooling tower and compressor erected, gas brought and pumped in system. Electrically all circulation checked before being utilized. Initially trials were taken on water so that no milk was wasted. Finally on successful trial of huge quantity of milk preservation was carried out. Immediately conveyor; hoppers and packing system installed. Aniket now thought of giving a brand name for packing of each bag. The Brand name was suggested by his father as Vijay milk and accepted by all. Next three months milk powder unit was ready. Boiler, water Tank with softener unit, Dryer vessel, conveyors installed. Powder weighting and filling machine in tins and sealing, printing everything was ready for trail. Additional milk from own milk farm house was to be used to make powder and tone milk; so that no adulteration would take place of any kind and to have long shelf life. This also had to go through the process of drug and food authorities of inspection. Even outsiders who were offering milk was checked for its fat contain and price was offered accordingly. Powder was given a brand name as a "Vijay"—a product from silver line—as producer and processor."

Addition to this Aniket added bottling plant. Bottles purchased were sterilized by the same hot water and steamed which was also utilized for dryer. This was how boiler was common for both processes. This additional facility with minimum cost was found to be more economical.

In same premises two storied office building was built up. Ground floor allotted for works. Part of it for workers dress change room and lockers. Others for supervisors and packing material, crates, and Engineering goods.

Second floor was reserved for commercial, administrative and marketing purposes. Neatly arranged offices could impress any outsider and also found comfortable for all working staff inside.

Aniket found that Anand was more interested in works and also milk—farm houses. As a part of production he was to take care of fodder produced, fertilizers and farm equipments. He too was assisted by a experienced manager who worked for production, storages and bottling plant. Top offices were well equipped with all facilities. He asked his sister Kalpana to take care of administration. She was graduated with personnel management from Delhi institute and use to be with her father on many occasion for various visits and meetings. She too asked to look after accounts and cash handling. Aniket himself took charge of marketing, visiting various whole sales and retail outlets for milk and its products, in most of the main cities. Even corresponding for export of milk Powder and tone milk. He too interested to manufacture baby food out of cereals and co-co. Some of the processes of manufacturing details brought from overseas by him for future development. He too employed one lady Assistant for marketing job. Her name was Shamala. She herself approached in his office and told him that her husband was working with modern dairy but due to his sickness he was no more. For few days she was employed in marketing department in place of her husband. She has to leave that job after two years, as company was locked out permanently. As she was in need and also had work experience, was given a job in marketing department. Quickly she could grasp entire system and never left her table till she completed all her work for that day. Shamala was very attractive and energetic while working. Anyone could notice how sincere she was at work. Some of the co-workers could remark,

"She must work hard. There is no other choice but co-operate with each one of them."

Once on some occasion Aniket was out of town and one whole sale dealer of her previous company contacted her and enquired about companies production level, kind of products and all that. She immediately talked to Kalpana and asked whether she could visit whole sale dealers office and bring this client to show our factory. Kalpana waited for a moment as she was unaware that some of our staff also can lead and take initiative. She allowed Shamala who went to visit client by company's milk van for duel purpose. She visited to his office. They recognized each other as she was working in marketing department in billing section. They discussed regarding modern dairy's failure and ultimate closure which was because of workers unrest. Some discussed about issues of workers, pending wedges and if someone was ready to take over that unit along with huge land to its surrounding. Then she spoke about silver line food product and its ownership. After getting most of the necessary information the owner agreed to visit the processing factory. As soon as both alighted from dealers car, she informed to Kalpana who asked her to take him around the factory along with Mr. Anand. One by one all units were inspected by the dealer who could gaze upon the total quantity of milk processed and product packed for sale. He never forgotten to check all licenses to manufacture and certificated by food and drug department.

"Let us have some tea and snacks in my office sir. I will introduce to you with Kalpana Madam, she is in charge of this office" leniently Shamal spoke to dealer who agreed. In fact Shamal did not wanted to waste this visit, took her to Mrs. Kalpana. Mrs. Kalpana was almost taken a back for a while, when she saw Dealer and Shamal was approaching to her. For Kalpana dealing with customer was new experience but could notice Shamal's confidence. Shamal was speaking to dealer like a professional and as a she was a part of this management team. Kalpana and Shamal offered chair to that dealer. Kalpana was graduated with MBA but when such situation aroused Shamal found to be more undependable and freely accessible to customer in her individual capacity. Shamal initiated talk while serving tea and snacks. She too could convinced the dealer how maximum quantity of milk powder and milk tanker and packing could benefit him. This entire discussion across the table was successful to fetch order of 20% of factory's production which would be lifted and sold by him. He too was prepared to get signed agreement on paper.

This was great success to Shamal who was congratulated by Anand and Kalpana.

She waited next day till Aniket arrived and took him to that whole sale dealers office. This professional dealer had a large network of many other product. He negotiated with the dealer till arrived at final price agreed by both of them. Aniket also formed the other network in addition, in a similar way what Shamal could sold through him. Aniket thanked Shamal for this and was too happy to give her added responsibilities of marketing. Day by day Aniket and Shamal got near to each other, discussing lot many issues for hours together in his cabin. Many occasions use to go out together for business purpose. Some murmur could be heard by Aniket's father. He is being Chairman he asked Aniket "Why can't you depute one senior person above Shamal. After all Shamal is Lady and wherever you go out she too joins with you in town. Even many time with you for meetings. You are aware of those town people who are jealous of our progress and our new set up. It should not affect our reputation and progress in near future."

"No Dad, it would not. I am sure people who are talking now, soon or later would realize. I know how she works intelligently. She is the most active, sits even late evening till her days work is complete. She went all around and brought all her previous Modern food product's old clients and even some good technicians for which we were searching for. Moreover she is looking after her in—laws even after her husband, death who was only a son to them. This was clarified by her to me. Even if she re-marriages would not leave them who are like the real parents to her! What more is required for her intentions. You too aware, my bonding with Jessica is forever. In my absence, I would like to make her a authorized person to sign all documents, even to take her own decisions."

Aniket daddy Dinanath thought over the matter for a day or so. He was aware of Anikets nature, once decided he would go through after some of his own analysis. This means he is not only kind enough to his staff but support them for their inherent quality. Aniket after his marriage likely to be away from this factory with Jessica who are professionals and would be progressing in that stream. They both had already proved respectively. Dinanath who was little upset earlier, bridged the gap of these thoughts said "Aniket, what ever you are doing is O.K. your views are positive in this regards, I support it."

—xxxx—

Jessica, and Aniket were in contacts on regular basis. She congratulated Aniket for his success that too within short period; though almost a year was passed. Aniket was happy to learn from Jessica that her four Tower Project was almost completed, except internal work would take another 4-6 months, meanwhile outside painting was completed. One of the Tower was to be acquired by Govt. officers was already handed over, though small work was left. In fact Govt. officials wanted to do the interior as per their choice. She wrote to him, "Aniket, all four towers sanction were received because of your architectural plan and yours initial follow up and its so happened that I could construct these 4 towers looking like huge pillars. Now a days it's a talk of the town. It really looking beautiful from our terrace. Even my dady and grand—pa could not believe that we could do this wonder."

Dinanath and Aniket together wrote to Samuel that "we are reaching your place next week. We will let you know the day and time of arrival of our flight. This time as soon as engagement is over, we would further decide the date of marriage possible therein your presence itself."

That was how Jessica on the terrace cleaning, keeping all plants in well shaped with cutter. Waiting sun to rise. She stood there might be first time proudly, looking at her four towers at west—end. Today Aniket was to come with his family members; but Aniket was being accommodated separately in Drawing room equipped with all, dining table, small book-shelf with collection of books purchased from various countries. Attached to it was the bedroom furnished with attached bath-room. New curtains, vaz in the corner was equipped with different statues. This was like a small museum with cool and fresh atmosphere. She collected some beautiful flowers and leaf, kept along with purchased pink daffodils at entrance and near his bed, made the atmosphere lightly fragrant.

Jessica, Jack, and Patrick all went to airport to received them with bunch of bouquet. Whereas Douglas and his wife were busy in preparing lunch and other requirement to get them fresh after that long journey.

Samuel was sick and day by day was getting weak as if very aged old person with wrinkles around. As soon as guest arrived, went and seen Samuel and enquired about his health. Some times he used to whine in night but unable to tell why? In spite of that Samuel looked happy and stared with his deep eyes at Aniket and raised his shaky hand, expressing everyone to go ahead. "All is well !" In vibrant voice expressed "you all get fresh and after lunch we will sit together and discuss about the engagement. In fact I wanted to have this ring ceremony at Jessica's official resident but she is reluctant to it. She wants to carry out in this house. I could not avoid and distress her. Distribute all responsibilities among yourself to complete this ring ceremony. You may decide marriage date with Aniket and Jessica's consent jointly as Marriage would to take place in India. This Jessica's wish that marriage ceremony should be held in Hindu Ritual way which she was very much impressed. Myself, Jack and Patrick do agree and positive for her sensitive feelings." All went to Patrick's home for lunch, went through the stud farm and took rest. After dinner Jessica and Aniket left to occupy his guest room. Whereas Jack, Anand, Douglas were planning the ring ceremony.

Next day early morning Jessica tapped Aniket,s door and asked him "let us stroll on my terrace garden. We will make nice coffee for us there. That is my favorite place. Every morning I sit there and enjoy early birds view!"

Both went on to terrace, were waiting to see the sun rise which already was being set in golden pink color. It was amazing to see as if its wings were spreading around. She poured coffee in both pots but Aniket could not hold himself sitting in chair, was amazed with beautiful site. Winters fog curtain was slowly settled or being removed slowly. He felt cool spring waves around. Jessica brought his mug of coffee and said, "Aniket, I could not believe this day would arrive in our life in Pink of color through cool breeze. As soon as one Golden pink is over we will see silver line at west side. Look it is already shining on all those four towers. Making our future strong and snout forever!"

"Yes, Jessica—this is real indication of our future!" pointing out at those pillar of togetherness and strength.

For ring ceremony Jack and Douglas were on their toes doing every kind of activities. Patrick and daughter in law were helping them, Samuel was taken to another arm chair in living room. Everybody was happy. Everything was arranged as they thought of. As soon as rings were slipped in each other fingers, Patrick exclaimed loudly.

"Our sky is one. What we have done today with help of Aniket and Jessica, the divided land by water is bridged together by their love. I congratulate both of you. "Aniket, and Jessica went to Samuel and Dinanath to take their blessings and then after Patrick's. Jessica was looking different than usual because of her orange sari and sandals which Aniket brought her from Kolhapur. He too was looking tall and smart in the dress purchased by Jessica with a golden color tie.

As the dinner was over, Dinanath with consultation with others decided date of marriage which was just after six months from that date. He invited all of them—must come there to India at least a week before so that all arrangement would be carried out in each others consent which was agreed by all. Samuels face looked very calm, but happy. The other day they were to board a flight to India, all of sudden they received a news that Samuel expired. All of them cancelled their flight and came back. Strong hearted Jessica could not hold herself, sobbingly told how calmly he breathed in last! Even after three—four days no one was in mood to discuss about anything but mourn. One could notice Jessica who was never seen ever before so much in sorrow in her life. She was continuously weeping. Jack, Patrick, Douglas could not control her. It was difficult time for everyone. She was mourning for a week. Dinanath suggested Patrick and Jack let Aniket be with her till she wants him here. Aniket would complete all her pending work before marriage could place. Patrick humbly thanked him.

All gathered at Church for monthly mass. Many unknown public too gathered as Samuel being Jessica's father, may be as news flashed all over. But Jessica was near her father's grave, offering flowers which were planted by him, and lit candles. Jack, Douglas too were with her. Aniket was never leaving her alone for a moment. As the mass was over at church many of the unknown youngsters and their friends and relatives put marriage proposal for her. Patrick & Jack intervene and told she was already engaged with Indian Architect a friend of her, and no more proposal from any one. Patrick published a news of Jessica's engagement in all news paper and likely date of marriage which would take place in India. Off course this was the talk of the town and in many other cities too! It was all that her all aspects of life were admirable and even for the engagement public praised her. Condolences and greeting both poured in together but Jessica replied in one word to all of them, that was "Thank you!"

Aniket drawn line of completion for all works she had under taken. Even he helped Jack and advised to Dominic's empire's executives by conducting number of meetings, found to be useful and helped Jack to work on that line. Jessica too decided to concentrate to re-build her—Samuels Dream House. She use to go everyday to her village and demolished entire house. She already kept plan ready quite long time before but her mother was died and Jack was in U.S.A. Samuel did not wanted to carry out any of such work over there though all material was stored in his premises. Sudden death of Jenifer made Samuel sad, so much that he lost almost all interest in his life. It was Jessica and her ambitious work kept him alive. He was never went to his field any more after that. All farming was given on contract. No more activities of construction or growing vegetables or farming milk. He was living absolute retired life, possible for his son and daughter. In spite of that he wanted to be alone till Jessica's engagement was over!

Since every thing was on board she put all efforts to complete her house. During work she could forget everything but again as night covered, she used to remember him and got in sob. As days passed, Samuel's Dream House was completed. She preserved their all articles like her mother's utensils and articles in the same place where it was. His arm chair in balcony with side table, over it spectacles with case. This prominent place and mark she decided to maintain. Whenever she visited she felt he was there waiting for her. Patrick, Jack Aniket, Douglas made that house as regular one. All appreciated Jessica and her deeds to keep them like a living memorial for ever. This brought her satisfaction of doing his that last wish in reality. Slowly Jessica turned back to her activities with Aniket's help. While working out costing of some of those projects were equally important for them.

Once early morning she decided to take stock of all pending work and material before completing this prestigious project. She opened the office—compound—gate herself. Before she could drove her car she saw one old but snout man possibly hanged over due to heavily drunk, and drowsy last night, holding news paper in his hand and waving at her to stop her car. Looking at his dark brown eyes, curly gray grown up hair and beard and dark brown torn over coat, could understand his edged figure. She got down from her car. As she went nearer to him. Started abusing her and Aniket.

"You both fools, greedy, rich people grab everything from us and leave us on roads to beg. What wrong we have done with you to make our this condition? You all are selfish working for yourself. Because of you my entire family is vanished. "The old man spoke in emotion, tears in his eyes. She called her watchman, asked him to take backside of the office where small garden and washing place was built up for workers working around. While giving him support watchman said to Jessica, "Since night he was laying outside of our compound wall. In spite of repeatedly driven away he came back here."

Jessica convinced him," Okay. he may be in distressed because of some incident and looking for shelter. As soon as he cleans all cloths and takes bath, provide him our securities cloths and over-coat. Give him some tea and bread which is available in our mess. Let him take rest till I come back from site."

He was taken back side of office. While doing so he dropped his cotton bag and news paper. Jessica took them and placed side of the wall. While doing so she noticed that was yesterdays news paper where, "Jessica's Tower a landmark of our city, equipped with all utilities used in modern Technology." She thought possibly this may be reason behind this for his anger. Another old news paper was protruding through his bag. That may be of his family photograph. It was publish of second World—War. The news of probably of his son who was while returning to his camp from his home town which was just on the boarder of camp site, was set on fire because of bombing. His son, too was victim of it. It was learnt from him that he too was helping army to supply tents and other material.

He further narrated, "I was impressed by those army people and asked my son to join the army who was victim to it. I lost all my peace of mind and everything. I do not know my purpose of living. I find too difficult to pull on for every day and waiting for the dark end of this tunnel." The old man said helplessly.

As soon Jessica came from the site, she asked for the old man. Instead of discussing further, she asked him whether he would like to stay in their trusts home and work there for children and help them as a security personal. He agreed and sent him to that home.

One of the office attendant came in informed to Jessica, "Madam, someone from the mayor's office wants to deliver a letter to you in person, shall I allow him to see you?" Jessica looked at Aniket in question, given permission to him. He handed over a letter, saying, "You may send reply in returned with me, if interested." and went back. Letter was containing that states International cultural and heritage departments secretary wanted to visit Jessica's office on 3rd day from today; at your office, in morning hours and requested to be available. It was also added that purpose of the visit to discuss on construction of museum. Both agreed and replied to do so.

Aniket rearranged entire office floor as required to receive them. Jessica brought all photograph of her and Aniket work. All were framed in glass and lined up in conference room. Some snacks and coffee was organized as expected members were not more than 5 to 6 persons. Jack too joined them though was not knowing exactly purpose of visit. Two vehicles parked in front of building and her office attendant brought them on first floor where office was located.

Mayor of city along with state secretary of International cultural department with his two assistants and one of their consultant from France also joined them. Mayor introduced Jessica and Aniket to everyone there who were present. Mayor requested visitors to go through the various department of that office like designing, modeling and execution. Requested to discuss on project of Royal Restaurant with market building and four towers which were on completion recently. Went through some of the administrative and costing files. Carefully seen all photographs and actual plans. Aniket was smart enough to gaze that some good project may be required to be designed and to be executed by Govt. that is why these officials are here. Keeping this in mind he explained them every corner of work till they were satisfied. Conference room was also well arranged and ready to receive them. All of them occupied their chairs. Govt. Secretary thanked all their office staff and Jessica and Aniket for their way of reception they arranged and appreciated work they completed in short period within budgeted cost.

Mayor informed Jessica and Aniket, "Our Minister in charge asked to these officers to visit renowned young architect who will be able to complete construction of museum task within 3 years at specific cost. Work will be organized by Govt. with help of charitable donor. Location will be near to the sea face, say, nearly 500 meters away from its shore. 40,000 sq.meter,. area will be allocated within that entire region where project is to be plotted. Secretary has about 15 such firms on their list to whom they are approaching to fit in, but only after finalize their design, cost, and duration of construction. List of specific material required for the project would be provided by the state government. We expect to receive your design with different views, cost and duration of its completion, earliest by third week from today. By the end of this month you are sure to get the results if you go through in all respect." Mayor and all other once again thanked them in courtesy. They all wished good-luck to them and departed.

Aniket and Jessica, both wrote some of the details on papers, were given by them. It was written,-The main objective of—the museum was required to show human races development and their cultural activities all over. No cast, religion or races was the aim. At the end special note was given that this museum is a monument that has to stand at least for 2000 years. Step wise inspection along with government staff would be carried out. As soon as they left, both put all files in their cabinet, except few which were kept inside their individual drawers.

Aniket pulled back his pending papers for completion, which were lying idle for last two days, but could not concentrate on his job. Same situation Jessica experienced. While on dining table at lunch—hour he saw Jessica in silence. Aniket could not hold back himself. "Jessica why we should not work for this new project? People approached us because of our previous work. There is no harm in working for it. I will give you some design and then we will select out of it okay."

Jessica reluctantly said, "I agree with you but I am not for it." "Why Jessica, what is reason"? Aniket simply asked.

She penetrated her eyes into his said vehemently,—

"Have you read the term of three years as a dead line for completion. More alarming to me the monument has to have a life of 2000 years! Its amazing. Even old experienced skilled person could not do so, in spite of support of renowned kings, in those olden days in their period. This monument is going to be a heritage to every one. It is easy to be social, help poor, organize trust but National trust building is a life long task which will be discussed by people ever after its completion for number of years with various remarks!"

"Jessica it's absolutely negative approach. I really do not understand a great lady like you can speak such way?" Aniket spoke in surprise.

"What about our marriage Aniket? That we have promised to each other." Jessica immediately put her query across.

Aniket replied softly, "So what is problem? Marriage will take place as decided, but this opportunity will never came again. I promise we will have scheduled marriage in India. We will have enough days before marriage and even after that we are going to come back here again and complete this, provided we win this project. After all we are yet to design and if approved then only all this would happen, till then we have enough time to organize ourself."

Jessica in acceptance said, "Okay. Boss Okay once again! I will assist you but you will be designing.'

Aniket in joyfully, said, "Totally agreed".

Very next day Aniket drawn sketch of the land which was 500 meters away from sea. Made square to match 44000 sq.mts area, there in plotted drawing in various ways to cover architectural view of 10,000 sq.mt that was one quarter of land and left over reserved for garden, rest-room, children's park for visitor. Entry, and parking drafted from various views. By changing location, various types of buildings joined together by over bridge, connecting straight to each other did not satisfied him. Separate blocks for displaying various aged and unearthed articles, earlier historical cultural segments from 10,000 years to 5000 years, 5000-2000, 2000-1000, 1000-500, 500-200, 200-100, 100—till date were drawn on paper. This classification was very important for him as historical sculptors, and arts would be located which would tell human progress with geographical background. Aniket found to be very clear about all other, except building design which would be a winning factor.

A week passed by without any decision on building. Jessica was observing him closely. One day she was to advice Aniket who was found to be restless, "Why are you to troubling yourself. We have many other work to complete" She could not hold herself. This act would have demoralized him that too at this time when he was living with sleepless nights. She could see from her window, late night lamp rays and shadow of his image moving to and fro the other side of dead wall to other wall. Next day morning he ranged up to mayor whether he was aware of the location of the monument to be projected at that sea face. Mayor answered him that he too was not aware of it, in spite of his repeated request to chief. He did not know even the District where that would be constructed. Truly they kept secret for every one of them. They did not even know the reason for that secrecy.

Aniket got it. He could imagine that could to be a busy street and important place but near beach. Possibly that land was kept under reservation for Government use. If this location was declared before project would finalized or, got through by Chief, it may happen that some another minister in charge, of other portfolio may try to take over. He might pamper someone to purchase that land by declaring un-reserved. Just as a last curiosity he could get Mr. Secretary in charge on telephone and asked about it. He too was reluctant to let him know, but could tell him," it's a beautiful and natural beach, has many palm trees around. This beach is a real holiday place for everyone. This Plot, both side have quite good wide roads. I hope this information is enough for you. No further enquiry please. I hope this matter is with you only. "Aniket thanked him in return.

"That's it!" He exclaimed, after keeping down the phone receiver.

Jessica was busy for completing Anikets, unfinished work of tower's and its surrounding development and getting through like solar system trial report and all that. She was purposely not going to his table to disturb his concentration in work.

This critical as well as crucial period prolonged for some time and all of sudden one day—

"Jessica . . . . Jessica . . . . I got it!" Jessica amazed at his shouting. She could see his happy smiling face.

Aniket explained to Jessica said "The Mayors secretary do not know the location. Though its where—about was unknown but what I could understand from him, the kind of surroundings of that monument. That is enough to put memorial as I wanted. Area had many palm trees. I want to match the construction of this building to sea face surrounded by those palm trees. Now there will be large three buildings in the shape of trees, means three ERA. All three trees, that that would be in the form buildings, would be taller than any other surrounding trees around. The middle one would be tallest where it's both side trees would be over lapping and shorter in height. Each of those trees would have straight vertical trunk. The middle one would have branches which would work as a link to the other tree or a passage from one tree to another and the last and like." Aniket stressed his proposed plan in confidence.

Jessica asked in doubts "What could be the base for it? It has to have a strong footing otherwise, how would it stand for 2000 years? Aniket, I think this seems to be difficult task, you may think for any other option."

"No other option, Jessica. This is the only way to have this memorial. This matches 100 percent to its surrounding, nature. This suits to all sensational discovery could tell us so much about the people lived at that time. What is architectural world? It retells us about past history, culture and heritage of ages in nature. Each tree will have one trunk to support in natural way similarly each building looking like a tree will have on trunk and its side branches to connect each one of them internally."

"Aniket, do you think this artificial trunk will support each building in tree shape. Will it be balanced with stormy wind or any earthquake?"

"Jessica give me some days, I will work out all loading factors. Middle tree will be taller so will have more storied and side two trees will be smaller, have less storied. Linkage between them would be built in branches to support each other. All three trees will stand in natural way in one line. I will do it Jessica."

Jessica too was intelligent enough to understand his plan but what kind of tree he is planning which could balance was unaware about it. That too for 2000 years, again was a question for her.

Very next day someone from Mayors office asked Aniket about progress in project Design. "Its already 10 days passed another ten days are still for you."

Aniket replied and confirmed, "yes, I am on the job, you may hear me within a week". "Okay. Best of Luck for you!" officer said.

Three day were over. Aniket asked Jessica to come in the designing room with some colors and drawing brushes. She too shocked to hear this outbreak. He showed its entire lay out. He was painting out every bit of it; right from compound, entrances two end, garden, children's—park, refreshment sheds, roads around, car-parking. Middle space was without any sketch.

Aniket requested "Now you paint all these lay out."

"But what about main monument?" said Jessica.

Aniket pushed three sketches to her side and said," These are three different sketches for you to chose. You may select any one of these and let me know best one. I know what you would prefer but I want to see once again whether our choice is the same. I also sketched common drawing of monument which we will be pasted latter to this vacant space."

"So much confidence about me, really?" Jessica happily appreciated the way he delegated such an important selection to her that too for which she was longing for. She pulled out all those lay out carefully."

While, Aniket turn around and went to bring another three cuttings of monument, said, "Yes, Now you complete your work I will bring all those three cuttings. You just space it over vacant place. Technical part and its calculations are with me. I know this memorial has to withstand in any condition of natural almighty at least for 2000 years and it will!"

Jessica strongly penetrated her eyes in his and he too raised his thumb before winning the race!

As soon as Jessica completed all layouts with paint, he brought three different cuttings of different trees. One with banyan tree having large spread over but number of thin roots protruding from branches as a support. The second one pine trees long enough pointing at sky and third one of three X'smas trees together but in one line. Jessica found x,smas trees comparatively smaller in its height than pine and banyan but possible to accommodate seven floors of normal height. Each floor had its branch bough were connecting to its side trees bough to support each other and also to bridge the gap in between them. Side trees could accommodate only 4 floors. Trunk of middle one was shown as 6 feet in diameter while side trees of 4 feet in diameter. Middle tree of around 75 feet high, while both side trees that were to its left and right of 45 feet high. Jessica selected X'smas tree cutting which was already painted in green and trunk in dark brown color. She pasted it on the vacant space over that layout. She found wonderful get—up with its surrounding. Spaces left in between leaves are nothing but all windows to make entire-floor airy.

Looking at that final sketch Jessica pointed out, "Is this trunk enough to carry such heavy load of so many floor?" Jessica asked in question.

"Of course, I have calculations and more over I have some other technique which will be ready within a day. The soil details could not be drawn so far which would decide how deep excavation has to be made before soling and concreting. Cost of excavation and concreting would be edge over the costing. If hard rock is found, then required to crack them, brake and make necessary wide deep bottom surface so that entire structure does not slip during any extreme weather condition. Now think that specific area is icy in winter. Structure is likely to shrink because of minus degree temperature and vice versa expansion in summer."

Aniket further added "Now, to take care of these seasonal changes which can affect other two adjacent side buildings. Uneven linear contraction or expansion can develop cracks in the lined formation of these three structures of uneven height. That is why I thought of duel type system which would not only could stand in extreme weather conditions but also last for thousands of years too! Middle trees trunk of 6 feet in diameter, though looks cement concreted and plastered from outside, the inside 3½ feet diameter will be of cast Iron filled in with wood. That trunk will be in 3 pieces, casted in star shape. Star's angular voids will be filled with shisam wood which has to be seasoned.Shisam would be stronger than Burma teak. These Shisam wood will be in triangular in shape to fill up star,s voids covering to form perfect round shape up to 5 feet high. This is how, cast iron star filled with conical wood will be part of the pillar. Such 3 pillars of equal in length will be bolted together to make one trunk. As soon as star shape pillar casted while that was red hot, the lengthwise triangular wood will fill the star's gap which will char the surface of wood while cooling down. This smooth ash would work as a sliding lubricant on expansion and contraction. After erecting all these pillars, branches would protrude at the joints in a similar way which will have minor effect of weather. Cement concrete coating of plaster will be done after formation of these threes structure. Trunk and branches will be carved while cement is wet, and thereafter would be painted in dark brown color to look like tree. These skeleton trunks and branches would be covered to form seven storey building and side trees will hold 4 storey each. Roof of all these each floor would be covered in green slanting leaves, would give X'smass trees look, and that spiral spire of top of those x,mass trees will give everyone a spiritual spirit. Voids in between leaves will be fixed with toughened white glass as windows". Aniket was speaking with his blue print in one hand and pencil in another, fully concentrating on his over-night prepared plan.

Jessica was just stunned not only by his imagination but also his thorough studied background. Its nothing but most intellectual out came of this project for her.

Jessica remarked in wonder, "Amazing! Anne, I never thought that this could lead you to such a solution!"

All plans, blue prints and its sketches of asthmatic views were packed in different cartoons. Costing and time duration within range was calculated and kept separately. Five to seven percent variation depending of site and soil details was clearly mentioned in.

He also mentioned to conduct a stage wise inspection from competitive person so that no delay occurred, while to be in schedule. After 3 days. he was informed on telephone that his plan was short listed and being studied by experts and shortly would hear about its results!

Jessica asked him to take some rest now and advice "Its too tiresome for you. I will make some break-fast for you."

While seating near the dining chair he remembered a line of a writer "Thou hast made us for thyself O Lord and our hearts are restless until, they find their rest in Thee!"

Jessica looked at his philosophical face and lines he murmured. He continued saying, "Adventure is in the Journey, not in the destination. And they say, it is not winning or loosing, but how you have played the game matters"

"Wonderful" Jessica cheered and clapped." This the right spirit, let us keep it up Anne!"

Third day he was informed on phone that they are sending a letter of acceptance, in returned he too would be writing the letter of acceptance of that heritage plan for museum.

Further added to this "Remember, This is also a memorial, and we all congratulate you for that! You may go through the letter of acceptance in which you would know, the exact location of this project. Location should be kept secret till foundation is ready."

He was also informed that other two competitors had very good plans but they lagged behind because of their exorbitant costing and longer duration of construction where as his looked smaller in size but quite impressive with novel ideas.

Super-structural arrangement would be a real matter of attraction to entire mankind. This super-structure of x'smas tree has proved a edge over on other competitor!

This was a red letter day for Aniket. He jumped and shouted "at last shrugged!" and virtually lifted Jessica in Joy. She too looked at him with sparkling eyes and congratulated him !

Jessica was delighted and spoke, "Aniket, right from beginning your were looking confident. This courageous nature, positive attitude, and the confidence brought you to this goal."

As soon as he received a letter of accepting his architectural design from ministry of International heritage and cultural department asked Aniket/ Jessica to visit to sign the acceptance of this offer in writing with the terms and conditions mentioned there in. Both of them drove to Ministry's office. They were honored and congratulated by Minister himself; along with the money—draft as a 1st payment for the preparation. Without loosing any time both went to the allocated location which was nearly 300 kilo-meters away from the place, of course, near the sea face. As they reached they found exactly what Aniket imagined. Its natural and beautiful environment would definitely to suit their planned project. "Simply beautiful" Jessica uttered. "Addition to our memorial it would be one of the best place on the border of France and Spain."

"Yes, Jesse, what I imagined, that the same now I am experiencing. Now we will prove on this too! No matter even if, time limit is bonding to us."

Aniket wrote a letter to his father that how he could get this noble project of monument work to prove self along with Jessica. In returned his father congratulated him. Dinanath further added," This contractual work would put you on heritage records. I am really proud of you my son. It is Jessica who is inspiring you all the time so half of the credit goes to her and her families who supported you both! Good Luck! Now for me your tying up with Jessica is also equally important. I suggest before you commission this project work, you all should come to India, get married. There after, you along with Jessica may go back and stay till work is over".

Aniket put forward this proposal to Mr. Patrick and Jack who too agreed to Mr. Dinanath's proposal and advised them, "This project work would take another 3 to 4 years for its completion, so it is better you both should get married. This will give a better prospect of real togetherness while working".

Today Jessica and Aniket went to Government Department, handed over the initial phase of preparation and also authorized Jack to take care in absence of them. Accordingly letter handed over to them. Initial activities charts were handed over to everyone along with Jack. Initial process was carried out in presence of Minister, and Mayor in charge. Patrick too joined them. Many workers were organized. All machineries were put in services. Big ware-houses for cement and for some equipments were built. Jack was busy in building site office. Aniket informed his father that "we all are prepared to come to India as soon as proposed date is conveniently fixed. At least one week before, would be good enough for preparations. After marriage at least a week would be enough to go around to visit some temples and get blessed. This is also a wish of Jessica. Here at the site, work was progressing in a good spirit and harmony. Jack was found in a full control of work and enjoying it too!".

The day of departure to India approached. All flew on the decided date and landed in India. Everyone was busy organizing some or other part of preparation. Everyone including Jack and Patrick were engaged in decorating hall and Pandal in open ground. Some Office staff from Dairy, and farm-house also joined them. Kalpana a office executive and Shamal were in forefront in arranging Jessica's various dresses for different occasion. She too preferred colored sari with Rajasthani designs and Mozzadi as footwear. Shamal was also given the additional work of catering, to be looked after.

Marriage news was already spread earlier and news channel were on toes being Aniket was to marry to a foreign—bride. This has promptly alerted every one which made to call police department to cordon the ceremony celebration without any problem.

Hindu ritual Marriage ceremony was very important for Jessica who wanted to note every chanting to be recorded clearly with Video shooting. This kind of keen interest she shown was not only just a fashion but to understand every meaning of that word chanted.

Many popular public personalities attended the marriage. Even some envoys from Delhi's foreign department were present, Show was worth of displaying on screen for which media too was active. This also could control the crowd in the vicinity. Jack was surprised by various dishes of various states were arranged for buffet. India's variety of food seems to him in rich in nutritious quality, smell of warm flavor could not hold him back. He and Jack tested every bit of it from all tables.

One separate pandal was erected for town people possibly many of them were even uninvited but made their presence. All were guest of Dinanath who too prestigious personalities over there to add glimpses to others on that occasion. Marriage was over in most exorbitant way and witnessed by all the town people as well as its surrounding villagers. News off course was published in all news paper, as was expected on the front page.

The other day Jessica and Aniket went to Rajasthan to visit the palace of Jodhpur and stayed for a day. Other day visited Jaipur and left for Ajmer to offer chaddar and flowers to "Dorgah" and sought blessing of the peer. This was like magnetic call of the heart. She felt unique experience when both bow down to touch the feet as a tradition to seek blessings from Dinanath, Patrick and other elders. She too do not know, but some sort of satisfaction was experienced by her.

Before leaving back to Spain, both visited Kolhapur's Mahalaxmi temple which was quite ancient and famouse for prosperity. Without fail Jessica's family made a point to visit a Kolhapur Maharaja's palace and Museum. It was displaying various items and photographs of many generations, including foreign kings and queens of England, France, Portugal who visited to them. What ever gifts were presented to them by various countries, in their honor could tell how great and able kings were they. One of them was highly learned from U.K. He brought coal engines and laid rail lines and commissioned the first railway in his state before British could do so in India. That was how he proved his capability and adoptability to modernize.

All of them were very happy after experiencing these Indians as open hearted and transparent in nature, and hospitality. Impressed by their ancient cultural activities which is rare anywhere else in this world. Even their common attitude to guest was uncommon. They are more receptive. Time was running short but no other go but to reach back to Spain. Before leaving, Jessica embraced to her father in law and also remembered her father. She felt as if she fulfilled his and Samuels wishes too! Then she went near to Mother in law's photo-frame, hanged on the wall. She offered flowers and lit a lamp. When Aniket,s mother was alive, she enjoyed her company, specially while cooking and learning many Indian recipe. Even Patrick, Jack moved for a moment. Her attachment to this house was natural still many unforeseen incident took place before this marriage. Nobody knows what way almighty had lead us!

On return journey everybody was in happy mood. All alighted at Brussels airport and then landed to Barcelona to drove straight to Jessica's home town. Now it was Samuel's Dream House. She plugged some flowers from the garden before entering the house and offered flowers and lit candles to her parents photo. Aniket and others too followed her. Even she went to grave yard to pray and lit the candles. Both stood there for a while, all of sudden Aniket noticed as tears were rolling through her eyes.

In full of sorrow and choked voice Jessica could spell out, "Dady, what you and I wished, was fulfilled by us. Bless us for every good did we do." That day was passed with many mixed emotions.

The other day both went to their official residence. But now Anikets guest room was turned into permanent joint room. She removed all luggage, arranged them neatly. She herself made some snacks, bread—sandwich and fruits juice for lunch. After short nap both were egger to go to the site. Jack already left early today to know the site progress. Jessica said, "Aniket, today I will drive to the spot. I do not know why but I feel different like a free bird. I feel to fly in the sky spreading wings lightly. I am really happy after a long time, achieved whatever I wished. I know you are more interested in this ambitious memorial, where as for me duel life is precious. I will help you but now would like to be more in a family life which I too dreamt earlier, but some or other situation continued to keep me in this profession. As they reached to the site it was almost evening. All workers were left to their barracks; even Jack too left back to town. Aniket decided to stroll on a beach, bare feet along with Jessica. He could see a pink large round of sun at extreme west-end, but so quite as if to say-good bye to that calm and silent sea and promised to see again, tomorrow. Aniket vehemently remarked "When everything is fine, progressing—everybody is happy. Look at me. I have my loving wife with me, warm bed and feasts but this is not a everyday life. When we see gusty sea, stormy wind, gusty high tides will be pushing us back many times to board, do not allow to swim but stay deterred at its bank till it cools down. Life is also like this. This is how this memorial monument has to stand for. This is the sign of progress in nature!".

Jessica sharply replied, "Aniket, I justify, you always speak poetic and philosophical but truth of the life. You are genius off course! I will be with you till earth remains, never deterred in any condition that I promise!"

In office Aniket was busy with 2nd phase that was to be taken in hand. That excavation and soling was the prime factor of foundation on which construction would be safe and sound forever. When he was organizing the crucial part of project in office, some outsider wanted to see Jessica in her office but she was away for some domestic work. Aniket asked to wait or she could see her some other time. In evening when Jessica returned to the office before going to house, Aniket could notice, now a day's Jessica looked quite busy herself on domestic front, informed her about visitor. He could notice her tiredness, advised her, "Jesse, keep some lady assistant to help you. Now you have many other activities and that is why some trained person is essential to help you."

"Yes, Aniket, I too thought over it before leaving to India. It would have been too early that time to appoint someone as newcomer. Person would have been wasteful without any work in our absence, being unfamiliar with procedural way, that we had built in. Today while going to market in that busy lane, I found a lady working there in one of the departmental stores. She happened to be in my office earlier, asking for a job. That time it was not required but I asked her to be in contact with me. Today, she reminded me there in that store. She is widow taking care of a only child who most of the time remains sick. She wants to give him proper medical treatment for which seeking better salaried job. I asked her to see me tomorrow in our office. We both will get conversant with her and then appoint".

Jessica was aware that after completion of this work someone has to carry on all these activities and help jack on day to day basis. She already thought of developing at least two persons who would sincere enough to continue to grow this organization. She also thought of having a lady architect who could manage professionally to help Jack who once also remarked to both of them. "You both will be settling in India then such a big organization would be orphan!"

That time she advised "No, Jack, no work should hold back, because that man in—charge is left for ever. See that Dominic's "Empire". How systematically organized. No way its progress is locked. Personification is very bad for any organization. One goes some has to come on that stage. Play must go on Jack!" Jessica spoke to encourage him.

Work was progressing, people and visitors going to sea beach could observe some construction work was in progress but unaware of for what. He was requested to be alert by secretary in—charge. Once he told Aniket. "A handful of selfish people will not be allowed to spoil national mission which is significant enough to shape as you set for!"

He too was cautious. He asked Jessica and Jack, "I think some small house should be built up here in this compound till work is handed over to authority or hire some apartment nearby."

All were of the opinion to hire a apartment. When crucial work would be in progress we all reside near the site because of long hours working and there after long distance travelling to our home, would exert.

Jessica and Aniket visited steel foundry named, Tata International Private Ltd., Spain. They spoke to their metallurgist and consultants. All details and drawings were provided of hexagonal pillars and quantity required. Purpose of the project was told without informing about location in beginning. Kind of metallic specification required to take up the load was discussed and finalized. That would be Spongy cast Iron which could stand to minimize contraction in winter and expansion in summer. Shisum Wood covering could control temperature would withstand with any kind of weather when supported by metallic structure from inside. Aniket gave them six months period including erection which was agreed mutually. Before filling black stones, all excavated portion covered with molten lead to observe shocks. Construction-work was over up to plinth level. Fencing, gate, roads work kept in progress. He planned garden around construction area. Accordingly sapling brought and some of experienced nursery's skilled workers were employed. Most of the variety of daffodils of his choice were planted in his presence. He was visiting this plantation regularly, before visiting construction area. It was a significant sign to welcome every person visiting there. As soon as pillars were casted and shisum wood shaped to fit in casted star to make it round. The construction team of erector brought all those pillar and accessories with them. This was heavy structure, brought by number of trailers, followed by one after another. Huge cranes were at site to unload those castings. The heavy truck moment was noticed by the public nearby. They became usual spectators for many days. Some thought of construction of big industry but why near sea shore. Some said may be civil aviation department at work. Some thought of sea navigator's control tower being set in. Many people, many gaze, could be heard. The great part that people working for the project too were unaware! As erection was in progress Jack and Aniket had very hard time to control all many activities. Jessica was asked to be in Town-office to look after commercial work, as lot many fund were received and to be deposited and disbursed. Invoices for various items and payment was also a hard task. She already deputed a Lady assistant Mrs. Karl to look after many other activities and assist her or regular basis. She too was in need of the job but after working with Jessica she too found out a way to succeed at work and developed devotion and concentration. She was satisfied for recovery of her son as Jessica helped her in getting through all kind of test and regular check up from renowned Doctors. Required medicine and health care was taken on prompt basis. Many times Karl use to bring her son with her who became used to all these staff members. Both son-mother found a new home, for them self, satisfied in all respect.

She—Mrs. Karl became quite close to Jessica, found kind lady in her. Once she asked Jessica, "Why you wear black pearls neck—less and two golden round halves at bottom of it?"

Jessica uprightly spoke, "Yes, Mrs. Karl, I, love to wear this Mangal—Sutra. In India every married women wears this. This is a sign of marriage for every Hindu woman. This is like a fortune to her and very precious ornament. It has a scientific reason too!"

Looking to her forehead, Mrs. Karl curiously further asked "What about red spot of your fore head? All these make you different than our community."

Jessica acknowledged her question, found to be happy to answer, "Yes Mrs, Karl, This red spot is called as a Bindi. This a pressure point of our forehead which makes the brain calm. And remember Karl, The community is only a way of life. Human and Humanity is the same all over the world. Religions may came and go but not a humanity on this earth!"

—xxxx—

Site was looking like a huge dinosaur in skeleton. Many children and public tried for a close look at that site. More than a year passed, some Govt. people used to visit and check the progress as a routine. They could notice movement of number of truck loads of cement bags and stones and bricks were arrived. Mason, carpenters moving around with all sort of activities. The slanting portion of the that tree branches everywhere, looking like a eagles wings all around. Somebody remarked whether these are ventilators for a boiler house? For some others that was like trunk, may be chimney and ventilators for it. Some body says, "Is it not looking like a big ship?"

"Are they building a boat like Titanic?"

Brick work was faster than expected. All most all windows were fixed every space in between leaves. Many passers surprised such a huge building looks like grand Hotel in three parts was standing only on three pillars.

"Its great!". Somebody surprised and remarked, ********** "I think they will support sides with the stones lying nearby or at least building side walls."

The work almost took a speedy movement. Branches were turned into passages from one building to another till all four floor. Top three floor of middle building were arranged with round stair case, around the middle trunk. Everywhere sturdy lighting points were provided. Light fittings were specially purchased from Italy with glazed glasses to have good reflection in night or in dark time to cover cloudy weather. As green color was painted to all slanting roof top till seventh floor, was looked like a X'smas tree—Trunks in dark browns color too looking lively. Entire plinth level covered with black stones. Now the complete structure was painted in green color looked as if real X's mass tree ! Much of the internals were yet to be completed. Minister in—charge asked to display a board at all corners of that area and write in Blue color as "Museum—Heritage". Down below by Govt. undertaking. Yet another year was required to finish the task. There was enough time to give finishing touch and for internal fitting. Mean while to make arrangement to display all brought out articles, write up, specimens was equally important. Public from distance places made this as a visiting spot while touring. Many schools and colleges buses were arranged special visits to this place. All foreign visitors from other countries also positively made to visit this place. This was because news spread as soon as board was displayed at that site. Whenever people strolled over to that beach, gather over here to observe this beautiful structure. Its a project of monument erected to know world the Heritage. This was a global memorial in the from of X'smas Tree. It stood among those palm trees. From distance it gave look of real tree. That site of three super structures was a real wonder for every one. As board displayed, public thronged around it. Children want to be inside but were not allowed till work was completed. Every Saturday-—Sunday people from various towns and cities wanted to see this super structure in the form of X'smas trees. Who so ever visited the beach, could see the structure for a while and then proceed. Every day the structural tree was becoming more and more attractive. News flashed in all news paper before the inaugural ceremony was to be performed. Before handing over that creation to Ministry of International culture and art cell, management ordered the statues and sculptures from all over world. Those were from Japan, Singapore, Malaysia, China, Burma, Nepal, Tibet, India, Turk, Arabic, Egypt, England, Italy, France, U.S.A. and Africa. All religions and saints statues, like Lord Gautama—Buddha (Siddhartha who was a king) who left his kingdom to become Monk, travelled from master to master with begging bowl, seeking enlightenment. As Gautama monk who became impressively asters. Instead of living in comforts he tried the opposite, solitude, sleeping by the wayside and subsisting on what every scraps of food he could beg for. It's still appealing choice because we equate austerity with virtue. Gautama became some—one entirely transformed—The Buddha. Same way great soul the Mahatma Gandhi, fought bloodless war against British Raj that was Satyagraha to get freedom for all. His philosophy of non-violence was simple living and struggle for Truth was well known in World.

kabir a muslim saint who was a spiritual traveler sung philosophy for common people. He said there is no substitute for first hand experience. Similarly Yeshu—Christ known for the same philosophy for peace and love for man—kind. He was crucified for his teachings. There could lot many things could be told which most of the people are aware.

For age-old culture which was found in Mohan-Jo—Dorro was symbol of ancient Indian's way of life. Ajanta—and—Yellora—Caves details, Egypt Pyramid—all duplicate arts were produced and displayed.

Bust statue of Swami Vivekananda was brought from West Bengal who was educated, mastered in Yoga, wore simple saffron clothes, and a turban on head. His strength of yoga, was well known. He travelled from India to America for religious conference. The religious conference was well attended by many countries religion head. The conference hall was over packed with people. Swami-vivekanand,s speech was suppose to be a very simple as he wore saffron color dress and a turbaned. When he stood, and looked at that gathered crowed, calmly said, "Brothers and sister of America.!!! "The entire spectators kept clapping and admired his kind heartily words produced smooth wave though out, gave a standing ovation by entire audience present there." These all were collected by archeologist and their age wise were arranged from middle Tree to others. One block of museum was reserved for present life style of all countries, to represent their present culture and how they live with that.

As days passed, every day some or other news paper was publishing Jessica's and Aniket's photographs, their work, even printed signatures which was found on one magazine, praised his work, wrote, "One Indian Architect's wonder—A Xmass—Tree in our country"! "Master's super structure!".

"A young Indian A Heritage for our country."

On the very first day of inaugural masses of uncontrollable public thronged inside the compound. State police had hard time to control them.

Finally they announced to the public, "from tomorrow we will keep this memorial opened for whole day. You all should excuse us for the day. Only specific numbers of visitors will be booked every day morning and no extra visitors, till we announce further!"

Both Jessica and Aniket, decided to go for outing at least for a weak. This was must for them, after working long hours—, days and also like years.

The Chief of international culture and heritage asked Mayor to have a small meeting with Aniket and Jessica, along with their relatives. "We will be calling some important dignitaries to honor them. Accordingly date and time could be fixed to gather in city's council Hall. So please request them to be present and inform us accordingly."

On hearing Mayors massage, Aniket—Jessica, both got astonished. That day Jessica took a lead to get prepared Aniket with her dressing choice. Chief Minister, Mayor, and many other dignitaries of social organization and President were present on dais. Mayor requested Aniket and Jessica to occupy middle chair there on dais. Entire hall was nicely decorated. Jessica's all relatives and friends, associates too joined in hall to congratulate them. Some press reporters were given a special chairs to give necessary publicity of that occasion and world monument. Chief Minister garlanded Aniket and Jessica and Mayor too honored them with bouquet, in India style and greeted them both. Crowd went on clapping and gave a standing ovation before chief Minister could give a speech about their creation.

Mayor made a statement to make aware publicly about this couple,—glanced at Aniket and Jessica vehemently, declared, "First let me congratulate both of them for their 3rd marriage anniversary!", Entire hall gone through a sweet shock wave out of surprise. Even Aniket, Jessica too starred at each other in great admiration!!.

"Yes, I collected all information about both of them, right from their childhood till final years of Architect and there after their work at U.S.A. We all are aware of her charitable trusts, agriculture school, building of Grain storages as a national interest and her prestigious towers at her town. She is from farmer family as Aniket is. His father was an ambassador born in rich family. Both were friends since long, helping each other in every projects they under took. Certain conditions made them apart but mystery brought them again together. There friendship transformed in relationship and that is marriage!!!. Today is the third anniversary and we all will be celebrating here itself on this dais where you all are there to participate!.."

Once again audience cheered at them and welcome!

All rose from their chair. Song that displayed for their future and well being. Somebody brought cake and asked both of them to cut. It was a warm ceremony of different kind in that hall. Patrick, Jack, Douglas and all became sensitive in emotion on that occasion.

When entire hall calmed down the chief minister got up. He emotionally looked at both of them and smiled. "Gentleman, Today is special day for me to honor both of them. This couple is extraordinary for all of us! Aniket, The Indian, shown his talent while executing the entire project. His way of approach to every problem he faced during execution were unknown to all of us but we were at close observation that no one disturb his projection of this global memorial. Skillfully and courageously he could progress. We found him sensitive but strong at his objective which gave him a pride for this successful achievement. Since yesterday I am receiving calls from various states and countries of this wonder of super structure in the form of X-mass—tree. Government has announced a package of prices for both of them, including permanent citizenship if he wants. Both are given a free world tour in various countries for five years!"

Some press reporter approached to the president of the organization to have some questions to this couple. In fact the organization was un—prepared for such question—hour. However Aniket looked at those press reporter, okayed to answer them.

"How do you received an idea of this X-mass tree for this structure". Reporter.

"Initially, I had no idea of such tree, but I thought its not only a national monument but global memorial where ages old historical culture and age wise heritage could to be displayed as a architect. Only architectural view or construction of large expensive building would not be enough. One has to see where it could be built. What kind environment and surrounding should be there. What kind of structure could be suitable and purpose of construction. Whether that for residential, commercial or public utilities. But this was a National museum. That was again a heritage memorial which required for detail study like how long it has to stand. As we see Egypt's pyramids or Mohan-Jo-Daro's culture in ancient period of India, speaks lots about its past. Similarly our monument should become worldwide famous for its super structure which can last more than 2000 years and displaying of various ages of human life in progress. This kind of work has to be embodied with special effect and that is what I done."

"Mr. Aniket Government offered you a permanent citizenship. what you feel about it."

Aniket said, "I am very much thankful for this offer and many of other incentives given to both of us. My work is recognized by authority for which I am very happy. There are many others who are also eligible for this honor who worked and extended help to me. Off course Mrs. Jessica and Mr. Jack are the main support to me."

A question from reporter, "Mrs. Jessica, how do you feel after marriage when your husband had hectic schedules of work?"

Jessica answered boldly, "Marriage is only a legal tie up for society. We were friends since long. We both would be friends for ever. This relationship keeps our bonds in the form of marriage which need not be affected because of any of us were, busy in work."

Same reporter asked further, "We heard that you will be settling in India as your work of this museum is over."

Jessica replied, "I married to Indian professional who is my husband. we both are of this opinion to be in India."

When other one asked, "What you feel about your mother land and India".

Jessica got the point of asking by the press, promptly answered "This is my birth place which will never be forgotten. I love my country and people. There is no question about it. India is ancient country. It has its own historical culture and heritage. It has many races, languages even dresses but there is a common link between them is their culture, festivals and worship and Yoga. The country was among richest country once upon a time. Ancient India had many education centre, where students from all over the world use to come there to stay for years and study in with all many faculties that is what we have equipped now. Arts and paintings in caves like Ajanta, Yellora are famous all over the world. These people are more receptive and tolerant towards human, animals and nature than anywhere else."

Once again immature question was thrown to her, "Jessica, what you think, do you fit yourself there?"

"In India, I will fit where Aniket's home town is. That is in Maharashtra, so I am Marathi. Maharashtra Okay!..", Answered Jessica knowing direction and way the question was.

Once again reporter turned to Aniket for further questioning.

"Aniket, you are a Hindu in religion, what you feel about it?"

Chief Minister and president objected this question, when all were gathered here for a special occasion to honor this couple and all about memorial and world heritages. He was also looked furious and felt devalued for which we all were gathered appraised the human races of all kind on this earth for noble cause on equality. But Aniket confidently stood up to answer this question.

"I will answer his question" looking at those members who were at dais. The hall, entirely became like a silent ocean and also were eager to hear Aniket. Jessica too was embittered at this question.

Aniket wanted to know the audience sitting there, said, "It is good question for me! Let me clear you, Hindu is not a religion. It's a way of life. Systems are formed for common people. What we talk about culture is created on the bank of Indus river hence Hindu culture thereby called religion. In Ancient period fire was important for human which was also kept lit continuously at places. For any ritual ceremony or chanting of Vedas fire is lit. Many cereals, grain, sandal—wood, oil, butter etc, offered to fire while chanting. Sound, heat and organic vapors produced in fire mixed with air, forms electrons and purifies atmosphere. We also pray Shiva-ling. Its small tom shape protrude out of round shape in stone. One side elongated. Entire this Shiva ling grounded on earth mostly near river, lake or pond in North South indirection. This is nothing but physics. This ling in North South direction produces microns are electrically charged which are received from the earth's magnet in North—South direction itself; in presence of water.

These Electronic waves in the form of rings are continuously flowing or releasing from the Shiva—ling. When we go nearby and offer water over it, these micro electrons directly enters in our body, there by balancing our inner electrons which keeps us alive.'"

Aniket continued, "Thirdly all Indian festivals are created on geographical and regional environment. This is a form of socializing to all communities."

He added, "Lastly India is place where worlds all religions were born and many of the saints are groomed over here. That is why world knows the India as a unique land of GOD!"

Jessica stood by him and asked reporters "any other question?"

"Yes, one more question please!".

This was from audience, who stood humbly, eagerly asked Aniket.

"Sir, you must be proud of this memorial that you have constructed and for this you are honored by the state. This will be one of the additional feather in you cap. Now question remains how do you feel about it."

Aniket amazed by receiving this question that too from audience but looked happy to answer.

"This architectural construction in the form of X,mass—tree is standing near the sea and going to stand in future too, in Compassion to give message of peace and love to human kind!"

Aniket won the applause of the audience.

They stood up and admired and cheered at the unique spirit of the couple!!.

This was another red letter day for both of them, and speared out from that premises and audience there in.

Jessica along with every one of family members went to Jessica's resident. The other day someone from office informed there was a trunk call from India, may be of Aniket's father, Dinanath.

Aniket called him back and enquired about him. In reply Dinanath acknowledged his spirit and work done by him, proudly said, "Hello Aniket, Yesterday Jessica already informed regarding opening ceremony of that monument. I am very happy that you have done a wonderful work which will be remembered by everyone who visits that place. I congratulate you and Jessica for that. It's absolutely incredible. You both have done it. It was a ambitious project. Yet I tell you that your ambitions should never be limited."

Aniket leniently accepted his greetings spoke to him, "Thank you Dad. Today, a special program was arranged for Jessica and me to celebrate 3rd anniversary of our marriage ceremony and to honor us for this unmatched work. They also offered permanent citizenship to me and for both of us, five years package of world tour."

Dinanath said, "Once again congratulations my son!!! Tell Jessica too for this. Yesterday Jessica was asking about every ones Welfare. She informed me that within a month you both are boarding for India."

"Yes, dad, we are coming soon to our home town but only after organizing every administrative and other left over work. All assets and planned projects will be handed over to her brother Jack."

"Fine, that the spirit" Dinanath supported.

As soon as talks were over Jack and Patrick talked to both of them.

"Aniket, and you Jessica, look, now you became public figure in eyes of entire town or say even countrywide. I advice you both please go to some unknown place nearby where you both can rest and enjoy some long waited holiday's."

Jack suggested the same option which Jessica too agreed and left to one of the island near Barcelona for a week by a boat. As they landed on a small harbor which was equipped with all facilities. Boating, yacht—racing, and fishing. Other end had a beautiful beach from where it was difficult to make out a horizon as blue sea and sky were looking a homogeneous. "Aniket look at that end. What a wonderful site is that. Can you make out a horizon. Its so homogeneous nature, like both of us. No boundaries for it. We too follow this natural indication of uniqueness!"

Some taxi-driver approached who took them to a cottage. Entire atmosphere was quite and calm may be because of thin population. Every house, cottage was far away from each other. They all were Separated by the farm in between.

Cottage's compound gate was opened. Natural garden with grass looked like lawn everywhere and violet, pink and yellow flowers were protrude their small heads out. On opening the door they found quite nicely arranged hall with sofa, dining table, with attached bathroom and small kitchen.

"Its beautiful to live here Aniket."

"Jesse, We should visit here whenever we come to your hometown"

"Yes, I promise I will bring you", said Jessica.

Kitchen was equipped with gas and electrical oven. She took out a small pouch of coffee, milk powder and sugar cubs from her bag. Both sat together in Veranda sipping that strong coffee.

After some silent space, Aniket said, "After ages, I feel relaxed today. Our minds are always trapped in anxiety and pain. This place is away from everything, freeing one—self."

"Yes, Aniket, I do, feel same way. Humans Journey takes place entirely in consciousness. A mind overshadowed by fears, hopes, memories, past traumas and old conditioning. Such place is like a paradise, a way to become free!"

"That's right Jessica what I always think same way you too! This is what ours oneness. Our union stands on natural wave length. God has given a way of karma to both of us. Its God's blessing to us!"

Occasionally both went for yachting. Strolled in children's park or went to club where artificial ski ground was made. Both wanted to learn skiing and enjoyed for two days. While dinning in restaurant in afternoon Two couples with child entered with small luggage hanging on their back. In half trousers, tracking shoes, woolen cap and long sticks in hand looked nearly tiresome. Aniket enquired tracker, "May I know from where you all are coming please?"

The tracker said, "We had been to the mountain which is about 15 kilometers away from here. That place is famous for tracker, even for children. On the top of mountain many tents are erected on its plains. They lent us on rent. One can enjoy 2—3 days there with nature. Why can't you both visit that place. That place is quite safe. you will there with many trackers moving around."

"Thanks. we may do so."

"Jessica let us arrange a trip for two days or we can stop over there for a day."

"No Aniket, I do not like to stay over there. As you insist we may start tracking early morning and step down on the same day."

"Jessica! it takes two hours to climb, then rest over there and coming down will be late and tiring."

"No problem, that can be done."

Next day early morning both tracked with some snacks, two full thermals of coffee and water bottles. As they reached on table plain area of that mountain, took a tent on hire, for some hours where they could lunch and rest. Both stroll around, enjoyed monkeys jumps from tree to tree. Trackers too wanted to be friendly with each other's by offering fruits and biscuits. Even they enjoyed the taste of various kind of juice were available. Different atmosphere in natural cold waves felt like in paradise. Specific area was prevented for children. That one point was, on slippery peak, difficult for climbing, which was also a echo point. Most of the newly married couple visit and hear multiple echo of each others name, called a echo point. More the intensity of sound, the multiple echo could be heard!. Jessica, obviously, was very curious to climb.

"Jessica you were little reluctant to come over here for tracking and now you want to climb this slippery peak? Read that warning—caution-board—beware of gusty wind before climbing.'"

"Aniket, where there is a will there is a way, I want to hear your voice and echo, there in presence of heaven!"

"Oh Okay. Then, you will not leave my hand while climbing even for a second. You may drink some water now. We will not carry anything else over there!"

Both made there way with all precaution holding each other's hand. When exhausted kept their arm on each other waist and again proceed. After an hour they reached where cold breeze was blowing their hair, that charmed them. Cheeks became pink, and eyes watery. It was good for them that fog was almost melted. Both reached on top of it. There was small portion of plain surface where only two person can stand. May be that is the reason why married new couple preferred this place to stand. They carefully stood on top of it, holding each in fear and facing the deep valley in front of them, waited till to recover from exhaustion. Aniket shouted loudly stretching his abdomen "Jessica,—Jessica—!!!", she heard seven times duel of echo, looked at Aniket with sparkling eyes. Now it was Jessica's turn but she thought how to make tie? Jesse, rigorously breathed in and cheered out loudly "Aniket—Aaniket—!!!" which went like a sharp shooting and received back. Aniket counted that 7 duel sequence of echo and pats her where she was too happy to respond, could see she was really out of bond.

Holidays were over. Their childish way gave them a new phase of life as if both were newly born. They too understood life is to live and enjoy.

On returning Jessica asked," when so many Indian songs are played everywhere and so famous, but you never murmured even once,

"Oh, really, I forgotten them long back. Song is melodious when sung in light heartedly," Aniket said in recipient.

Jessica convinced him, "I understood that. Now there is free air for both of us. Let me here you!"

He thought for a while and spell out some lines. He said to Jessica, it's for you." SUNDER TAN, SUNDAR MANAH! TU SUNDARTAKI MURAT HO!" means you are too beautiful as your soul is. Truly its GOD who made you so beautiful, "Aniket sung few lines further. Jessica was too glad to hear him," Oh is it! I did not known that "said humbly."

Both reached at their resident in late evening in different mood. The other day, drove to her village home where Patrick Jack and Douglas joined them. "Jessica, you are really looking too young after these holidays. You both are completely re—freshed.I could see original charm on your face. Good! We all want you both should remain in light enjoyable mood forever!"

"Thank you grand-pa, we will.'" Both uttered at a time.

Both of them looked confidently to each other. Jack and Douglas too wished them to have same kind of trust in each other.

Days were nearing to proceed for India. Another 2-3 days were left. Patrick and Jack, helped them to collect all necessary documents and sculptures and gifts. She did not forget Aniket,s trunk which was with her containing all his books, that was left earlier by him.

For her all useful gifted articles, her favorite dresses, gowns and books were bagged by her. Many other baggage filled in to give some memorable gift to present to her father-in law and sister too.

Aniket informed on telephone from his office that he would not be available for today's lunch. He was busy in re-arranging all office work there. More over one of the architect who worked with them earlier for last project was appointed by him to help Jack. He would be in charge as a director over here. Your office-in charge worked for accounts, purchases, and administration, that Mrs. Karl was also present. She would be a administrative executive to help Jack also. Aniket reconfirmed whether the said organized management was acceptable to every one of them and also did not forgotten to convey Jessica who in return satisfied with that arrangement.

Jessica informed Aniket, "See, I am going to village with one bag of some articles which were brought for my Dad and grand-pa earlier. I may stay over there for the night."

Further she added',

"Tomorrow only after lunch I will be back here. Our cook and maid would not leave till I came back."

Her this visit was prior to leave for India while many thoughts were lingering in her mind, when she left for her village. She opened compound gate, looked in the garden and went near to all those plants and daffodils. Touched them in emotion. Then to the ice—flower tree which was planted by her mother Jenifer and nourished by Dad. Samuel too was fond of when the tree blossoms. Tree witnessed lot many ups and downs of this house but still stood in smile. Cook came running through the door—, collected the bag from her, was kept near the door which was already seen, kept open for her. This was the only living sign remained for this beautifully renewed Dream—House. Neatly arranged, strongly once standing in its glory but now found empty! She sat in Veranda instead of going inside. Found neat and cleaned. Instead of going inside she preferred to be there in that veranda. This evening was quite for her today. Otherwise lot of activities in this compound, made everyone on toes those days. Going and coming inside with baskets filled in with vegetables and fruits. Somebody was bringing green fodder from fields. Mother was in hurry with milk cane and jars to milk the cows. Dad collecting farm articles and storing them in backside warehouse. As sun sets and evening spreading its wings; Jack and she used to be here helping every one whatever way was possible. Every-day, late evening warm fragrance, indicating cooking was in progress. Jessica was as if sensing the same as everything still lingering to her mind.

Those days, she used to go to kitchen to know the kind of food being prepared and like to help mother the possible way. Dad after a warm water wash would go to Balcony and sit in his arm chair. Now she got up as her cook in kitchen was preparing a dinner for her. For her, Jack and Jessica were, now a day's regular visitors at every week end to this house and now added by Aniket's presence to make this dream—house more lively. Additional members of Jacks wife and children made the house more happy home.

For Jessica, Today was a different day. She opened her bag. She removed sets of dishes, plates, bowls and designed spoons which her mother wanted when she was alive. That was purchased by her long back. But after mothers sickness she thought improper to bring it here. Now it was a time for her to leave all of these utensils here in this house, in her memory! While going up through wooden stair-case she found some places were nailed by her dad. There she hanged two painting and one statue of angle in corner shelf. She Similarly, for hall brought two beautifully wooden carved clocks. Out them one was, dark brown in color and another one with pendulum which was purchased earlier by her to present her father as a birthday-gift. She looked at it and hanged that one in drawing room and another in balcony. Sat down near the arm-chair; where Sammuel loved to be sitting for hours at latter stage. She swing that arm-chair, looking at it felt as if he was in the chair, discussing to her and blessing. In emotion she hold the chair with both hand and stopped its swinging. For quite a long time she sat there till maid came to ask for a dinner. Her restless mind after the dinner made her go up and down for some or other reason and finally made her sit in balcony till late hours. That night was sleepless for her and quite too.

The other day morning she again got up early before sun rise. Birds were flying as usual and crisping as usual. Cows and other animals were moving all over. Farmers too were hurry in their daily chore. But here Jessica was in empty mind standing alone in balcony for quite long time looking around as if for the last glimpses. She went down calmly made her coffee and again sat over there but nothing was charming her. Slowly with great efforts stood there for a while, mechanically came down looking once again at that dream—house and all around in a heavy heart. She locked her house; shut that compound gate and went straight to grand-pa's house. "Well came to you, Jessica. I was knowing you will visit us and this place before you leave. Yes child, is everything ready before departure?"

"Yes, grand-pa, Most of the baggage's are packed and ready., Aniket is at our office with Jack. New architect is also appointed. He is busy with office staff giving all instructions."

"Good enough, after all Jack has to take care." Patrick said in support.

"Yes, grand-pa, you and Douglas too should visit frequently to keep his morel in boost and know everything is in order."

"Yes., Jessica, when you leave this place ; be happy and do not worry for all this. Remembering all those old memories will make your life miserable. Enjoy now your own life ! Also let me know as soon as everything is set over here!"

Patrick could understand her duel mind and responsibilities she was leaving behind for all of us. But he was aware that Jack was capable to have a hold on everything. The other day she let her village in heavy hearts, looked in deep warm memories while passing her school. kept her eyes staring there. Next day at her official home at the time of lunch all wanted to discuss many other issues but Jessica could not concentrate on that; because she thought this would be a last lunch together with grandfather. Her eyes got wet in emotion!

In the afternoon she straight way went to her kitchen, Balcony, Bed-room of hers and went up the terrace. She went to all those loving saplings and plant. She cleaned those after cutting all old branches of sapling which were grown around with plenty leaves and sprinkled them with water. She checked all tools in position and sat for a while in chair. She glanced at her those four prestigious towers stood like those grouted strong pillars, in grace!. She herself relieved and she thought why should be in grave? Life is relay—one has to hand over the stick of authority to other and so on. That was what she was doing since last few days. Off Course one could not avoid sensitive emotions for close and dearer one. We should always remember them and forever, that would not stop the flow of any river stream. Every rivulet naturally flows to ocean finally. This thought immediately released her from all emotions. She was matured knowledgeable lady still she had to experience the thrust of life.!!!

Cook reached the terrace for menu for the dinner. Jessica asked her to wait and took her around the terrace garden. Told to her, "Look how I taken care of all these plant on day to day basis like a baby. Similarly I expect you to keep them growing. That box is containing pesticides and spray pump. You can mix that with water and spray once in a week. All tools are kept underneath. Whenever I visit here I must see natural good site here."

The cook accepted and said; "Okay. madam, what about kitchen and other rooms?"

"You need not do anything there, except cleaning occasionally. You can work for Jacks family that would be good enough! Today I will cook myself. You may take leave for the day now." Jessica said in comfort.

"Sorry madam, today I wanted to be with you please" cook.

Jessica understood her sentiments and allowed to be with her.

Jessica reached kitchen, went through all the cupboard after a long period. She took some vegetables for Indian preparations and belled some routes for her and Aniket. After all this was a like practice for her. Other day morning Jack, Aniket and she went to "Happy Noble House". All staff and trainer, teachers and students had news of her last Heritage project and there after likely to settle in India. More information they got through the news papers which made ex-student to keep in contact to this school and about her visit, so that they all could meet her. When she entered the school premises; along with Jack, and Aniket. all of sudden all of them gathered near her to congratulate for various reason but at the same time in grief that she is leaving for India with her husband. It made every one to think about her future. She addressed and met every one of them, talked to them and assured to visit whenever she is here. Once again she gave confidence to them, said, "Mr. Jack will be taking care of you all and this Noble Home." She continued,—"We assured you all help to all of you to become more confident to become individually independent. Always look forward to progress every day and keep up same spirit to work and learn together. Today you notice all our ex-student are independent and doing very well! How they are freely living in this modern and competitive society. They are your guide line. Follow them, they too are with you. "All ex-student raised there arms in acceptance.

"Yes, madam we are there." That was loud but in depressed tone was heard. One small but lame student was noticed by her; head down; in tears rolling, speechless, still stood in silence. She immediately rushed to him, took in her arms emotionally. Holding him for quite some time. This was once against difficult moment for her. She too wept virtually. Jack came running and took the child from her and patron him. Entire mass emotionally charged. Aniket too moved kept gazing the situation.

"This what Jessica is!. She herself is a love for all. She instead of teaching others, love is induced in every one," some one of member uttered.

Jack and many other members assured Jessica, "Jessica, do not worry, I will be informing you regarding all these student regularly" There after Jack and all of them left from there.

Then they visited their 200 acre agriculture land and farm house, students barracks, and their mess. She addressed them. "Look many of you are already became professional and learnt lot in farming technique. There is still much to achieve ; before you settle down in your family, bring them up economically. I am sure Mr. Jack will be with you, even Mr. Douglas is also a very good to organize your daily work if you want so. Within few years you will get your cottages build in that new township till then you can manage in this farm houses which are also being built up for your families."

All were happy to hear this declaration for which they were always very anxious!!

While going to warehouses and storage system they dropped on the way to see whether whatever was built up to plinth level was intact in that township project and what could be future course of its development. She informed Jack, "Whatever discussion is being going on among some traders for this new township is seems to be encouraging. This may click within few months. There were news in favour.Our plans for school, community centre, Savage system all are approved by top authority but foul play was not allowing us to proceed. That too will be cleared shortly. Jack you have to be very clever and strong during execution of this project."

Next and last visit was for grain-storages which were professionally organized. Head of technical and commercial background professionals were handling efficiently the entire system. This was also supported by State Govt. Its success remained assured as National Project. Jack was nominated as one of the director in charge and head to look after overall accounts and purchases.

In late evening all were at dining room in Jessica's house. Aniket felt disturbed and in mood of apology, said, "Jessica, I could not visit your village and Patrick too! In those days, in our early youth, I remember, how we both used to be with your parents farm. Then we would go through the fields, plucking fruits from trees, helping farm workers to cut fodder, bringing vegetable filled in baskets. I would never forget those days. I always felt at my own home that time."

"O.K. time schedule is not allowing us, but Patrick is coming tomorrow to visit you both, even to see you at air port."

"Oh, that is nice."

All luggage were kept at one place by Aniket, Jack and Douglas. Even their families were all there to help around to see nothing was left behind. Patrick also came there and sat quietly in a chair observing everything.

He got emotional while speaking to all the members in house, "Today Jessica is leaving the entire empire that she erected over here. Its not that easy to leave years effort that brought up her favorite trust and farms. Her village—house is like heaven for her. She is really a good child for Samuel and Jenifer. She has given not only support to them but also name and fame to them in every respect". Suddenly he rose and embraced, blessed her, "God Bless you and Aniket too!" she was in surge of sudden emotion and became speechless at that moment.

All came down with luggage. She remained back and stood for a while looking at everywhere. She locked her kitchen, bed-room, drawing room and guest room and was pushed in deep sorrow wondering when she could visit here again. All were waiting down below for her. As soon as she reached down there she requested to just to go to the office for a while which all followed. She went through all department and shook hand with new architect. She talked to Keri who became oversensitive and could not hold herself; and wept. Jessica took her in arm and assured "You will be always safe and do not feel you are an employee of this firm but you are in home. You will be taken care in all respect, be confident. You may write to me when ever you feel like. Is that right!"

Finally she went to her cabin looked at every small articles and material she used for her projects. Casually opened table's drawer where she kept her parents photos. She collected it and kept in envelope to carry with her.

Her presence in office always remained a driving force for everyone. They had drawn a great motivation from her which was the success factor for her organization.

At the air port many people gathered from various places to see both of them. Many engineers and even government officials, mayor, Dominic's—empires—all senior executives and other office staff but surprisingly many villagers and teachers too were present to see her off. Immediately she went to them to greet them.

They both accepted their good wishes and blessing.— waved at them.

She once again returned to embrace her grandpa who put his palm on her head to bless! She also embraced in emotion to Jack, Douglas, his wife and children, and joined Aniket to board the plane.

They both sat quietly in their seat without any talk for an about hour. Snacks and drinks were served. Both were seeping drink mechanically. Aniket broke the silence; spoke without looking at her; "We have to re-activate our consulting firm : A.J. Architect at earliest after reaching to India."

She just smiled lightly.

Aniket asked, "What are you thinking and why you are so quite!".

She simply replied, "Nothing, no thought at all".

"Is it a love from West to East!"

"Yes, It is!"

Their Plane was passing over the clouds, lands, rivers, and oceans current too!!.

Kept flying higher and higher!

—xxxx—

THAT IS HOW THEY KEPT ON THEIR WINGS
SPREAD FOR EVER.

—WINGS THAT SPREAD******!!!—

About the Author

Ramesh N. Sangle born in Nasik in state of Maharashtra near Mumbai. He started his career in Mumbai-as Mechanical and Electrical Engineer. He worked in railways locomotive workshop. Also worked for various projects. His last project was to manufacture-poly-iso-butene with technical know how from Argentina, (U.S.). Presently product is used to avoid air pollution produced by all automotives in India. Author is still working as consultant for environment.